CHRIS ROSSBACH

RED DRAGONFLIES

AND OTHER POSTCARDS

FROM HEAVEN

ALMACOURT BOOKS

RED DRAGONFLIES AND OTHER POSTCARDS FROM HEAVEN
published by

ALMACOURT
B O O K S

For information
ALMACOURT BOOKS·754 Apalachee Dr. NE· St. Petersburg, FL 33702

Confidentiality
The names of the patients, their relatives and their healthcare providers described in this book as well as many of the specifics of their presentation have been altered to maintain confidentiality. In some instances, details of two patients have been merged to create "composite individuals" in order to protect their privacy.

Library of Congress Control Number: 2015916702

ISBN 978-0-9969032-7-1 (paperback)

To My Wife

VIVIAN

"Hope" is the thing with feathers
That perches in the soul,
And sings the tune without the words,
And never stops at all.

EMILY DICKINSON, POEMS

Contents

PROLOGUE

Five angels burst onto the scene in the dreary room with gray-tinged walls and empty prospects. Jayden saw them immediately and described them to his father. "They're just sitting there," he said casually. When asked what they look like, Jayden answered without hesitation: "Pretty."

Most of us earthly humans may never get a chance to encounter a messenger from heaven, let alone five. What made things even more extraordinary in this particular instance was the fact that Jayden, eye witness to the heavenly hosts, was blind.

I started working at Jayden's hospital shortly after these events took place and learned from a coworker what had happened. In *The Little Prince*, Antoine de Saint-Exupery wrote that the eyes are blind and that one has to see with the heart. I suppose Jayden did exactly that. He was four years old at the time and suffered from congenital tumors in both eyes that had robbed him of his vision very early on. The disease was spreading throughout his body despite aggressive therapy. Twenty-four hours after witnessing this astonishing gathering, Jayden embarked on his final journey. I presume he did not travel alone.

People who reflect on their most memorable journeys often discover more about themselves than about the heartbeat of foreign nations and the souls of distant cultures. In the process they may very well realize, to their delight or to their dismay, who they really are and who they want to be. Without a doubt, I fall into this group of unintentional discoverers.

More than thirty years ago, I began such a voyage that I did not plan and did not bargain for. Allow me to take you on a retrospective through the most unforgettable moments: the haunting and the surreal, the dream-like and the divinely inspired, and the instances when separate lives intersect, never to be the same again. Sit back in a comfortable chair, close your eyes and dare to get out of your own face right now, as one of my young patients once commanded me to do. You may find your preconceived notions shattered, the boundaries of your imagination stretched and the horizons of your world pushed far into the distance.

Now envision I hand you a gift-wrapped package that you shake back and forth a few times to elucidate its contents before you conclude it must be a book. Inside you find your old dictionary, the one you may have owned since high school but have not opened for quite a few years. More or less in the middle of the book you come across this definition:

Medicine—a collection of beliefs that relate humanity to the supernatural. Wait a minute, you think, this does not make sense. Medicine and the supernatural have nothing to do with one another. You quickly turn a few hundred pages to corroborate that assessment and, to your surprise, you find another definition: Religion—the art and science of preventing, diagnosing, alleviating and curing disease.

In disbelief you study the book's cover and glance at the first few pages. Did you shake it perhaps a bit too vigorously and jiggle the contents out of order? Did you forge these pages, you may want to ask me, or fabricate absurdities to substantiate whatever preposterous argument you have set out to prove?

Let me assure you that I have no point to make. I set out on my life journey without a specific agenda, other than trying to be as good as possible at what I wanted to do. It is not the destination that matters, you see. It is the journey and what you do while you are on the way that does.

Conventional wisdom has it that science and medicine on the one hand, and religion on the other, are separated by a wide chasm that divides study, empiricism and knowledge from belief and faith—the latter often characterized as blind. I want to show you that looking at them as if they were detached or at odds and alienated from one another is folly. The Hungarian philosopher Thomas Szasz identified this imprudence from a historical perspective when he said, "Formerly, when religion was strong and science weak, men mistook magic for medicine; now when science is strong and religion weak, man mistakes medicine for magic." Clearly, neither approach works particularly well and neither satisfy the human mind and heart.

I first set out to make people physically better. I wanted to eradicate their infections and alleviate their pain. Later, after I specialized in the care of children with cancer and blood disorders, that included the cure of leukemia and various tumors. I may have fallen into the same trap that Szasz identified, and mistaken medicine for magic. A former boss did once accuse me of practicing what he referred to as "voodoo medicine." I know what he meant. It sounds a bit scandalous, but more about this later.

In hindsight, I recognize that many of my patients have made me better.

I am who I am because of them, and I'm not sure I've ever thanked any one of them enough for what they taught me. It's because of them that I can better appreciate the preciousness of life, the quiet moments of understanding without words, the need for perseverance in the face of seemingly overwhelming adversity and the simple gift of a smile and a thank you.

The stories in this collection are not mine alone. They belong to my patients and their respective families. I consider myself privileged to have been invited into their lives, to walk with them for a few days in some cases and for many years in a few others. I have tried to record their experiences as faithfully as possible. Some of my patients may even read these pages. I ask for their forgiveness for any accidental misrepresentation, although nothing written in these pages, as far as the core elements of these stories are concerned, is a figment of my imagination. What amazes me is the ingenuity and resourcefulness in the minds of even the youngest children, and the marvelous vision our Creator held in *his* mind when he fearfully and wonderfully knit them together in their mothers' wombs. If these stories intrigue and touch you, the reader, I have done the job that I think the Lord wanted me to accomplish.

It has not been that long ago that I needed to return to my hospital one Sunday afternoon to say good-bye to a teenage boy who had died, not unexpectedly, from complications of a brain tumor. A torrential downpour and peals of thunder gave way to a warm and tender sunset. Peach and pink colors diffused the rain-cleansed Florida sky. As I drove and wondered what I could possibly say to comfort his grieving mother, a most gorgeous rainbow appeared in the distance. About ten years earlier, another patient of mine traveled to heaven on such a blazing arc and later returned to tell about his remarkable experience. I did share that story with the mother that afternoon and saw a radiant smile where only tears flowed moments earlier. I have often told this story and many other, similar ones over the years, until finally, one of my friends encouraged me to write them down. "People have to read this," he said. I don't know whether you *have* to, but I hope these accounts may give you solace and comfort during times of suffering, or enable you to lift up a loved one or a friend during the inevitable darker moments of life and the *"valley of the shadow of death"* the Psalms point out. There *is* life after that, more life than you might have ever fathomed.

ONE

JESUS' EYES

Incomprehensible that God exists,
And incomprehensible that he does not exist.

Blaise Pascal, Pensées

He is no fool who gives what he cannot keep
To gain that which he cannot lose.

Philip James Elliot

Prayer opens eyes, ears and hearts and bids God to enter into a believer's life, but the Lord does not always wait for an invitation before he takes matters into his own hands.

The stories you are about to read span more than thirty years, five hospitals and two continents. They range from my first steps in medicine during work as a nurse's aide in an adult intensive care unit to very recent experiences in a hospital for children with cancer. But they share one common theme: our God is real and personal. And there is never a question of who is in control. May these accounts be a blessing to you!

Let the little children come to me, and do not hinder them,
for the Kingdom of God belongs to such as these.

LUKE 18:16

Jim Elliot apparently never questioned his decision to enter the mission field in the jungles of Ecuador, despite the extraordinary dangers such work entailed. In the end, he gave his courageous life when a Waodani warrior impaled him on a spear. Elliot's journal contains the quote on the preceding page for which he is known best. His mantra has inspired generations of those serving the Lord in far-away lands.

Thousands of miles away and decades later, a little boy at the tender age of three years knew nothing about Elliot but he gave us an inkling of what Elliot meant when he alluded to a relationship lasting into eternity.

Colin sat propped up on his stretcher, waiting for his treatment to start, and could not stop talking. He was cute as a button and well aware of that fact, so center stage came naturally to him. Dr. Bradford, his pediatric cancer doctor, had the reputation of a conscientious and respected physician. I have met him on a few occasions and I have never hesitated to contact him or his team for advice in particularly difficult cases. He loved the little boy almost as much as he did his own children. Nurse Andrea, who had known Colin since his first visit, took his vital signs.

Colin suffered from neuroblastoma. This tumor can be very aggressive. It typically occurs in the abdomen of young children and often spreads elsewhere in the body as in Colin's case. After several rounds of conventional chemotherapy and surgery, Colin had been receiving immune protein therapy, and with each infusion he experienced fevers, hives and terrible pain. His parents wanted to continue the therapy at all costs because they feared the disease more than anything else. During each treatment, a crash cart with emergency medications and an anesthesiologist stood by in case things really got out of control.

Soon after the twelfth infusion began, the pains commenced as well, despite a hefty dose of a narcotic medication. Colin's mother took him in her lap and bounced him up and down as she had done during the prior days because the rhythmic movement somehow distracted him enough to ameliorate the pain. All of a sudden, she felt him go limp. His lips turned purple and a grayish blue spread over his face.

"What's happening to him?" she panicked.

A severe allergic reaction rendered Colin unable to breathe, and Dr. Bradford could not feel a pulse. He turned to Andrea and yelled, "Stop the infusion and get me his emergency meds. We need the code cart!" Colin's father shook him, to no avail. They placed him back on his bed. Trembling in fear, his mother backed into a corner.

"Where's the oxygen? We need an Ambu bag," the doctor shouted. Sweat pearled on his brow. "Lay him flat," he commanded. Dr. Bradford started mouth-to-mouth resuscitation. "Call a code and start compressions," he exclaimed between two breaths. Andrea pushed a button on the wall and began to compress Colin's chest.

People swarmed in to assist in Colin's care. One of the nurses escorted the parents out of the room so they would not have to witness the increasingly frantic resuscitation efforts. The mother took one last look at her horribly discolored son before the curtain door closed behind her. She felt like crawling into a cave. Panic and disbelief hung suspended in the air.

The anesthesiologist could not place a breathing tube into Colin's trachea because his throat was swollen shut. From outside the room, Colin's parents heard him shout, "We need to trach him." He wanted to cut a hole into the trachea to allow Colin to breathe. By now, at least ten minutes had passed since he lost consciousness. The curtain flung open as yet another team member entered the room. For an instant, Colin's father caught a glimpse of feet sticking out from beneath a mob of people. Too long, he thought, too long. They should have gotten him back already. "God, please," he whispered. To everyone's horror, the code cart contained the handle of a knife but no blade. One of the nurses exclaimed that she measured no blood pressure in Colin's arm.

"This is not how this ends," his mother moaned. Suddenly, with a conviction utterly surprising to her, she added, "God, if this is your will, I'll be OK. I get it, God."

Minutes stretched into an eternity. A cacophony of voices suggested nothing but disaster until finally a first positive comment rang out. "It's faint but I can hear air go in and out."

The parents were allowed back into the room. "He's got a heart rate and he's breathing but it doesn't look good," Andrea said softly. People stepped out of their way. Dr. Bradford sat on a stool next to Colin, wailing over his swollen and almost unrecognizable body. As if frozen in space, his mother stood in the middle of the room, paralyzed by fear. His father noted grim faces all around and clenched his fists. No one said a word.

The doctor wiped his face with the sleeve of his coat. "I'm so sorry."

"Tell me he's going to be OK," his father begged.

Dr. Bradford hesitated. "He didn't have a heartbeat for a long time. I'm afraid he'll never speak or walk again. He won't be the same Colin you knew."

"Never?" his mother muttered. Dr. Bradford shook his head.

"What do we do now?" his father asked. He glanced around the room, searching for answers among his defeated audience. Nobody replied. "There must be something."

All of a sudden, a rustling from the bed caught everyone's attention. Colin stretched and opened his eyes. "I'm so hungry," he said.

"Colin!" his mother shrieked.

Dumbfounded, his father answered, "I'll get you whatever you want."

"I want chicken nuggets with barbecue sauce!"

Dr. Bradford asked Colin whether he knew what had just happened.

"No," Colin answered. He propped himself up on his elbow, checked all four corners of the room and asked, "Mama, is Jesus still here?"

By all acceptable, conventional medical criteria, Colin should have been neurologically devastated. The human brain is exquisitely vulnerable to oxygen deprivation, and Colin had been without adequate oxygen for quite some time. Dr. Bradford was not far off the mark when he predicted permanent brain damage—yet he missed it entirely.

Four years later, Colin continues to garner attention the moment he enters the room. I saw him a few days ago. He is as spunky and quick-witted as ever, with nothing in his speech or behavior to suggest he ever went through this ordeal. The office secretary offered him two little trinkets from the toy box instead of the usual one.

"Finally," he blurted out. "It's about time somebody here does something for the kids for the holidays!"

It's Christmas time that I'm writing these lines. Do you ever wonder whether Christ is real? Or whether he came down to earth two thousand years ago? Does he come even now? Read on. You be the judge.

I have set my rainbow in the clouds.
GENESIS 9:13

Mike was only a year older than Colin when our paths crossed while I pursued subspecialty training in Seattle. Without a question, he loved his parents and cherished his home. After his journey to heaven, he would have given anything if someone had told him he didn't have to return.

A cancerous muscle tumor in his arm grew back to such monstrous size that his shoulder froze stiff despite chemotherapy and radiation. Simple tasks of life such as eating, dressing and brushing his teeth posed considerable challenges. After about a year and a half, aggressive treatments to cure his disease gave way to palliative care and pain control. His parents agreed that if his life was going to be all too short, at least it should have a measure of quality and dignity. Mike did not want to linger in the hospital for days on end, attached to an intravenous drip and nauseated by futile attempts to shrink his tumor. Instead, he preferred to walk the beaches of Puget Sound and smell the salt of the sea. We had also talked about one day standing on the snow-covered summit of Mount Rainier, which occasionally broke through thick clouds, and we wondered how far one might see from way up there. His parents made the decision to take him home.

A few days prior to his death, Mike did not come downstairs for dinner. His father called up to him three times with no response. Fearing the worst, his parents scrambled up the stairs to his bedroom. His mother shook Mike, believing he might have died already.

"Mike!" she panicked.

Mike aroused from his sleep with profound anger. "Why did you have to call me back?"

"It's dinnertime. You've slept for a long time," his father told him.

"So?"

"Why are you so angry?" his mother asked.

"I didn't wanna come back!"

"Back where?"

"Here."

"You didn't go anywhere, Mike. You were sleeping. You had a bad dream. It's all right now." She stroked his head, trying to soothe him.

"It wasn't a dream, mom." The angry frown on his forehead vanished, the deep furrows around his nose straightened and a sparkle of joy spread over his face. "Mom, Jesus called me. He sent a rainbow down from heaven."

"A rainbow?"

"Yeah, for me! I climbed up the rainbow and I didn't have the tumor anymore. And I could move my arm." He rubbed the aching, disfigured shoulder. "There were so many children there."

"What were they doing, Honey?"

"We were all playing together when Dad called me. Now the rainbow is gone."

"Oh Honey." His mother did not know what to say. She looked to her husband, who sat down on Mike's bed, put his arms around him and sobbed. Mike died peacefully two days later. He didn't have to wait long to play with his new friends again.

On the opposite side of the world, in southern Germany, my report of Mike's experience elicited a variety of comments from my family when I returned to the old country. This sounded like a good story. An interesting dream. The fantasies of an excitable child.

Only two days later, we visited the *Wieskirche*, the beautiful "Church in the Meadow". In the background, the Alps rose into the azure sky. In the foreground, a Bavarian onion steeple and pearly-white walls contrasted with the surrounding lush green foliage. Inside, a simple white cupola was suspended above the elaborate Baroque décor of the church. Jesus stood at the zenith of the cupola, above the most gorgeous rainbow ever painted. The arms of the rainbow reached from the heavenly ceiling towards the nave below as if they were natural extensions of Jesus' body.

The majestic sight sent a shiver up my spine. I remember asking my family whether the appearance of the church didn't remind them of a story I had recently told them. It did perhaps make people wonder for a brief moment but it failed to enable anyone to see with the heart.

They will not need the light of a lamp or the light of the sun,
For the Lord God will give them light.

REVELATION 22:5

In the adult intensive care unit I had my first exposure to clinical medicine during my studies at the university. I signed up for occasional twelve-hour shifts at night-time as a nurse's aide. This work allowed me to gain valuable experience and at the same time make a bit of money to support my meager funds. During one of these shifts I met Keith.

He was by no means the first grumpy old man I had ever met, nor the only one with a broken heart, but he set a precedent when he returned from the threshold of death with a mended soul. When I talked to him later, his convictions dumbfounded me. His successful resuscitation forced him to prolong his earthly existence. For him that represented a curse rather than a blessing. I expected the opposite. Few people get a second chance, but that was clearly not his desire.

I remember well when I met Keith. Matted salt-and-pepper hair stuck to his head. Dark rings spread under his tired eyes. His wrinkled skin lacked luster, and three-day-old stubble sprouted over sunken cheeks. A long line of gauze pads with tape crisscrossed over them stretched from his flabby neck down to his belly. Ugly holes that were mercifully invisible underneath the gauze marked the sites where plastic tubes drained the wound secretion's bloody froth. Aghast, Keith held a mirror in his hands. The sight of his face scared him, for he almost did not recognize himself. He was sitting up in his hospital bed for the first time in days.

Marion, his nurse in the intensive care unit, was eager to cheer him up. "Back among the living?" she asked with a pretty smile. She knew he had experienced rough days following his open-heart surgery, although most of the time he had been too drugged to notice anything around him.

"You call this crap living?" he croaked. His voice sounded hoarse because the breathing tube used for surgery had scratched his vocal chords. He coughed and then screamed in pain, pressing his hands against his chest. Sweat glistened on his forehead. Marion took a wet cloth and wiped his face. "Slow, deep breaths," she said, soothing him.

"Thank you," he answered with a tortured grimace.

"You OK?"

"I guess I'm gonna live."

"Yep. You'll be fine."

"That's easy for you to say," he countered.

"True."

Scratching his head, he continued, "I want to shave. I look awful."

"Sure. I'll bring a water basin, and you can shave in bed. Or you can sit at the sink. Your choice."

"You think I can get up already?"

"Of course. That would actually be a good thing for you."

Marion lowered the bed and helped him into a wheel chair. She handed him a kit with a comb, a toothbrush, tooth paste, shaving cream and a shaver. He sat comfortably next to the sink, water streaming over his forearms. Splashing a handful on his face, he muttered an appreciative "Ah" and lathered his beard with a generous portion of shaving cream.

"Good?" Marion asked.

"Good? You gotta be kidding. This is great," he responded, elated, "I feel like a human being again."

"I'm glad. I'll be right back." Marion stepped into the hallway to get an antibiotic from the pharmacy cabinet. A sliding glass door between Keith' and my patient's rooms stood wide open, and therefore I witnessed the encounter.

A loud, hollow thump brought both of us instantaneously into Keith's room. He lay slumped over the sink. Tufts of shaving cream spread over his ashen gray face like ice floating in the Arctic Ocean. We could not feel a pulse and he was not breathing. Marion yelled for help. We wheeled Keith back to his bed where the resident physician inserted a new breathing tube. Marion started chest compressions, while another nurse injected medications into Keith's intravenous catheter. The monitor showed a heartbeat as rapid as a race horse at full speed. Three electric shocks and a host of medications did not suffice to reverse this gallop. After thirty minutes of resuscitation a normal rhythm finally reemerged when the defibrillator jolted Keith for the fourth time. His bruised and ravaged body regained its pink color again, but that simple change certainly did not guarantee anything. He had momentarily escaped danger, though he was not out of the woods.

Marion collapsed on a chair in a corner of the room.

"You all right?" the physician asked.

"Yes," she responded unconvincingly. A cold shiver ran down my back. Whether this came from tension, fear or relief, I didn't know.

Three days later, Keith appeared better than I had anticipated. I had not seen him since his awful crash in the ICU. His clean-shaven face exuded a healthy color. With his hair washed and combed, he looked like a new man.

"How are you doing?" I asked, glad to witness this remarkable turn of events.

"Better. Thank you." He somehow did not sound credible.

"You were lucky a few days ago."

"I'm not so sure." He looked towards the milk glass window that separated his room from the outside world, as if he needed confirmation or comfort from somewhere else.

"What do you mean?"

"Well, I'm thankful for what you guys did." He glanced towards the monitor above his head. Rhythmic blips indicated a healthy heartbeat. "But I wish you hadn't done it," he added.

I was stunned. I expected Keith to want to leave the hospital, rejoin his family and get on with his life. Instead, he expressed regret.

"I don't understand," I said.

"You have no idea. It was so beautiful. I saw so much light." He paused, shaking his head. Then he continued, "It felt so warm, so comfortable. I can't describe it. I didn't want to come back. Now I have to be here." He sighed. My face must have expressed consternation, for Keith apologized. "I'm sorry. I don't want to appear ungrateful."

We talked a while longer, but to my disappointment Keith could not be more specific in his description of where he had gone. Yet nothing could have been clearer: as dead as he might have been, he had felt sublimely alive.

Keith's comments raised a kernel of doubt in my mind. I considered myself an agnostic at the time. Mike's heaven-bound journey on the rainbow watered and sprouted that seed. Later, when Miriam came along, it matured into a beautiful plant. I was given faith by grace, faith only the Lord can endow.

Come to me, all you who are weary and burdened,
And I will give you rest.
MATTHEW 11:28

One early spring morning, seven or eight years later, I felt like Mike had sent me a reminder of his glorious encounter.

Halfway down the hallway of the children's cancer ward, a middle-aged man slumped against the wall, tears running down his face. People either did not notice or they did not acknowledge him. He was not a parent of one of the children who were hospitalized at the time. I searched the recesses of my brain before I remembered how I knew him. His eyes flashed recognition instantly.

His daughter Miriam had received care in our hospital until she transferred to another facility a half year earlier. Bit by bit, inch by inch, a synovial sarcoma, which is a rare bone tumor, mercilessly and cruelly ate away her left shoulder. Miriam went home to receive palliative therapy under a hospice group and died a month later.

"Hi," I said as I walked up to the man. "It's not easy to come back, is it?"

"No, it sure isn't."

"But it isn't easy to not come back either?"

"I had to come and see."

"I'm glad you did."

"Thanks," he nodded. "There are so many nurses I don't recognize."

"We've experienced lots of changes, for sure. How have you been doing?"

"Always up and down. It's hard."

"Did things get any easier for Miriam in the end? I know she suffered such incredible pain."

"No, it never got better. She always hurt so bad." He described his daughter's groaning, her futile attempts to reposition her body to find relief, and the frequent dose increases in the narcotic medication. His heavily distorted facial expression mirrored his daughter's suffering right in front of my eyes.

"Did the infusions in the arteries help at all?" I asked, referring to her adult oncologist's prescription of chemotherapy infusions directly into the larger vessels feeding the tumor.

"No, we never saw a response," he replied.

Unexpectedly, he perked up.

"We arranged for hospice care when they discharged her from the hospital. They came during the day, but at night my wife and I took turns taking care of her. Miriam was often so out of it that she couldn't press her morphine pump. Whenever we heard her moan, one of us would get up to help her. One night my turn came, but my wife said I should rest and she would go. I slept the whole night long. In the morning I questioned her why she hadn't asked me to help out. You know what she told me?"

I shook my head.

"She said she saw Jesus when she stood in the door to Miriam's room."

"Jesus?"

"Yeah. She described him. He wore brilliant white clothes. He pulled a chair over to Miriam's bed and sat down next to her without saying a word. When he put his hand on Miriam's arm, the pain went away." He outlined his wife's description of Miriam's calm, rhythmic breathing without her horrible moaning of the prior days.

"What did she do?"

"I asked her that, too. She went back to bed and slept the whole night long."

"What happened to Miriam?"

"She didn't have any more pain that whole night."

"Wasn't your wife flabbergasted?"

"No. She knew Jesus would take care of her."

We talked a bit longer, celebrating the better moments of Miriam's life, especially the unusual turn so close to its end. Her parents are forever grateful to know that their daughter is in good hands.

I do not doubt that *He* came that night.

I am the way and the truth and the life. No one comes
To the Father except through me.

JOHN 14:6

Having just read about Miriam's astonishing night-time interaction with Jesus, you probably won't be surprised to hear about the encounter another one of my patients experienced only a few months ago when I was finishing up this collection of stories. Half of the hospital knew Carlos, a seventeen-year old young man with an unbreakable drive to live and a dogged desire to follow the Lord. He had been battling a vicious tumor of his bladder for an entire seven years. The list of his chemotherapy medications, surgical procedures and radiation treatments could fill a whole book.

Last August, Carlos was dying. Everyone knew it, and so did he. Carlos talked about two important goals in his life, which remained unfulfilled. Foremost, he wanted to survive long enough to see his uncle one last time. He had been separated from him for quite a while. The uncle lived in Grenada and planned to arrive within a few days. Secondly, Carlos also wanted to die in the hospital, but his parents were making plans to take him home with them.

On Sunday, three days before his death, Carlos reported he had seen and talked to his cousin Carina. His father believed his son to be confused and gently told him that he must have meant Felicia, another cousin of his. Felicia, who is alive and well, had been visiting frequently throughout the last year. Carlos insisted he had talked to Carina. That caught the father by surprise. Carina had died a year earlier at the young age of eighteen months due to complications of abdominal surgery.

On Tuesday morning, his father handed him a medication. Carlos appeared to be on high alert. "I need to take that medication so I won't die," he insisted.

"Yes, I know," countered his father, yet Carlos' forceful response seemed out of place.

"Why is he standing in the door then?" Carlos asked, quite agitated.

His father glanced at the half open door. "Who?"

"Jesus. Can't you see him?" Visibly upset, he continued, "He needs to go. It's not time yet." His father sat speechless.

Carlos got his second wish, though sadly enough, not his first. He died in the hospital the next morning shortly after five o'clock. I said my good-byes four hours later. I have witnessed many dead children and adults—too many. But nothing in my past prepared me for this one. Carlos' face expressed the most beautiful, serene and peaceful smile I have ever seen. He certainly did not resist when Jesus came the second time around. What business here on earth did the Lord allow him to take care of in the twenty-four hours of deferred time? I don't know, but I suspect those hours must have been precious and important enough.

Months after Carlos' death, I happened to talk to one of the nurses who had been most intimately involved in his care. After I mentioned my plan to publish a book about my experiences with the children in our care, she asked me what title I had chosen. My quoting it left her shaken. She said Carlos had told her he wanted to return to this earth as a red dragonfly.

The foundations of the city walls were decorated with every kind of
Precious stone. The first foundation was jasper, the second sapphire,
The Third agate, the fourth emerald, the fifth onyx, the sixth ruby, the
Seventh Chrysolite, the eighth beryl, the ninth topaz, the tenth
Turquoise, The Eleventh jacinth, and the twelfth amethyst.

REVELATION 21:19-20

What images come to mind when you hear the word Florida? Disney World and the Space Shuttle? Sharks and alligators? Hurricanes and the Everglades?

More than twenty years ago, I found the Sunshine State awaiting me with open arms. I've met acceptance and inclusion from the first day I set foot on this remarkable peninsula between the Atlantic Ocean and the Gulf of Mexico. Its greatest strength, I have come to believe, is its people. I could not fathom how much of a melting pot Florida is. Whether "crackers" from Frostproof, migrant workers from somewhere in-between Okeechobee and Okefenokee, Buddhist Hmong from the highlands of Cambodia, atheists from China, Creoles from Haiti, Muslims from Palestine or the United Arab Emirates, Guatemalans or Maya Indians from Mexico, I have met them all. In a way, I have come to know the world—and its diseases—without even leaving Tampa Bay.

One little boy I want you to meet was even more of a newcomer here than I am. Abelardo was five years old when he arrived from Cuba a few months before I saw him in our clinic. He and his parents found freedom, only to discover that he suffered from an incurable brain tumor. We ruled out the surgical removal of the tumor because of its location. Chemotherapy would have been utterly ineffective and radiation could only delay the inevitable. His parents tried blue scorpion poison, which they imported from their native island. I didn't know about this rather unconventional medication, but unfortunately the substance did not help either.

Hospice care allowed the family to keep Abelardo home for a while, but when he developed breathing problems, he returned to the hospital. It became abundantly clear that he would not survive much longer. His parents were desperate. When I asked whether they could claim any spiritual connection, they stated they did not have any interest in religion. As I quickly learned, Abelardo had never attended church, either in Cuba or in the States, and as far as his parents knew, he did not have any exposure to Christianity in any shape or form. Abelardo's father stroked his wife's shoulder and back. She in turn sobbed inaudibly, her body shaking in quiet despair.

"I'd like to ask you whether I might share a brief story with you," I said.

"Please," his father answered. His mother nodded silently. In a few short sentences I described Mike's journey on the rainbow to heaven. While Abelardo's mother wept into a tissue, his father stared at me, his eyes piercing mine. I wondered whether he might be angry with me for talking about another child when his own could die at any moment, and I even entertained the idea of discontinuing my report before its conclusion, but then I decided to take a chance and complete it. He kept his eyes focused straight into mine without wavering one bit. As soon as I finished, he said, "Can I tell *you* a story?"

I didn't know why, but I knew what was coming. The way he said that gave me goose bumps.

"Go right ahead, please," I said.

"About two weeks ago, Abelardo asked, how much longer? His mother told him, you'll be fine. Several days later he pointed to the ceiling. When his mother asked him what he was staring at, he said he saw beautiful colors like large blotches covering the ceiling. Then Jesus came to him through these colors, telling him that he shouldn't worry because he would take care of him. His mother asked him what Jesus looked like. Abelardo said he had long hair, a beard and deep, dark eyes. The way he described Jesus' appearance, it was the eyes that had the greatest impact. His mother wanted to know how dark they were, and he answered, you know, darker than mine."

JESUS' EYES

Abelardo's Cuban, Hispanic eyes were indeed dark. I can't wait to see the Lord's eyes.

Before I formed you in the womb I knew you,
Before you were born I set you apart.

JEREMIAH 1:5

Beautiful Olina spent the first few years of her life in a large Buddhist family in Laos. She came to the United States at the tender age of eleven years.

Pallor and bruising developed over a period of a few weeks, and her parents brought her to medical attention. For reasons unknown, her bone marrow revealed nothing but empty spaces, as if one day it simply did not want to work anymore. Conventional treatment failed to heal her disease. Olina could not survive without a marrow transplant. She had no siblings who might perhaps have given her a new bone marrow. Her parents were not suitable donors, and an international search did not turn up any matches among several million unrelated donors either. Few red cells and platelets circulated in Olina's blood, and she required transfusions with increasing frequency. Despite a lack of white blood cells, she had been blessed so far for she had managed to avoid fevers and infections.

One rainy afternoon, Olina sat in a reclining chair in the cancer clinic's treatment room, watching blood drip into her intravenous line with the numbing rhythm of a slowly leaking faucet. The endless transfusion bored her. A video blared on the TV screen mounted on a shelf at the other end of the room, but she ignored it.

Her parents sat next to her. "Can we talk?" her mother asked when I stuck my head in the door.

"Sure. How are you doing?"

"Good, thanks. Can we go somewhere else?" Whatever their concern, they apparently did not want to bring it up in front of their daughter.

"We can go to another room if you like," I said.

Mr. and Mrs. Phab followed me down the corridor to an empty room. I closed the door and waited. Mrs. Phab faced her husband briefly as if to muster strength. Then she turned around with an exuberant expression. "I'm pregnant," she said.

"That's wonderful. Congratulations. How many months along are you?"

"Three months already."

Mr. Phab shook my hand. "Can we find out whether the baby is a donor?" he asked.

"You mean in general or now, before the baby is born?"

"Yes. Right now?"

"We could test the baby soon. That's certainly possible, although you have to know that this doesn't come entirely without risks. Of course we wouldn't be able to transplant Olina until after the delivery. Assuming the baby is a match."

"Still, we'd like to know as soon as possible. If the baby is not a donor, can you help us get an abortion?"

The request caught me off guard, and I stammered a few senseless words. It took me a while to add with a bit more strength and conviction, "We'll test the baby after the delivery, but I can't help you get an abortion. I'm sorry."

Olina was fighting for her life. More than likely, she would lose this fight without a transplant. Yet despite this desperate scenario, her parents considered the new baby worthless and dispensable if it turned out not to be a donor. They found one child precious enough that they wanted to leave no stone in her treatment unturned, yet they considered the other an inconvenience at best.

After wrestling with their predicament for a while, the Phabs decided to keep the baby. Konane entered this world as a healthy girl, and her cord blood matched her sister's tissue type perfectly. The transplant normalized Olina's blood counts, but it came too late. Before she turned thirteen years old, a fungal infection of her lungs ended her life. Olina died in the hospital.

Her parents stood at her bedside next to the chaplain who had known the family ever since Olina's first admission. She lay peaceful on fresh linens, her eyes closed and her arms folded over her chest. Tranquility replaced the labored, rapid breaths and the anxiousness her face had expressed for so long.

"Where, in your belief, is Olina going now?" the chaplain asked. Both parents shrugged their shoulders in silence.

It is difficult to witness children desperately cling to life, only to see them glide away mercilessly. Perhaps there is a spark of truth in the Buddhist belief that letting go of everything is the key to sanity.

If nonexistence is a reality in some oriental religious systems, were Olina's parents aware of it? Did they agree? Did Olina's death make her more or less real?

Nothing in life exceeds the terrible pain that the loss of a son or a daughter elicits. Such a death destroys the natural order of the generations; it makes no sense. Worse, one might imagine, is losing one's child forever.

The first of the four Buddhist *noble truths* is readily comprehensible. To live is to suffer. The small world of a children's hospital gives ample proof day in and day out. The second truth, desire as the ultimate cause of suffering, is also plausible. Did Olina's parents suffer because they had allowed themselves to get overly attached to the illusory world of their first-born child and, in pursuit of that, had they desired too much? Was she illusory only now, on her way to the grave and the nothingness and self-extinction, or had she been illusory all along? If her parents could not extinguish the yearning for their child, as the *third truth* implies they ought to do, would they suffer forever?

"What will you do with her body?" the chaplain asked. Apparently, the parents had not contemplated this issue. "You and your family could have a celebration of life," he added. That suggestion brought a smile to the face of Olina's mother.

Life, I'm convinced, is more than an illusory vibration detracting from what some people believe to be the fundamental nothingness of our existence, and Olina's parents must have thought so, too.

Years later, Konane is a growing, lovely little girl. Her parents are making every effort to keep alive in her the memory of her courageous sister.

You knit me together in my mother's womb. I praise you because
I am fearfully and wonderfully made.
PSALM 139:13, 14

Does God have an opinion about such matters? Reading Jeremiah or the Psalms, among other books of the Bible, you might quickly get answers in the affirmative. For my wife and me, he came up with a very unique response, and we were utterly unprepared. It all started with a visit from a German friend of ours whom I shall henceforth call King Herod, for privacy's sake as much as descriptive purposes.

Darkness fell quickly that day. The moon's radiant face reigned over luminous skies, but no star led the way in the east. An ordinary evening matured into the wee hours of the night.

King Herod lounged in the Jacuzzi. He had arrived after dinner. Small talk gave way to more serious issues he himself introduced into the conversation. I was tired after a bad call night the day prior and went to bed around midnight.

Before long, blistering questions rained down on my wife, a hail of sanctimoniousness and torrents of accusations. How can a good and just god stand idly by at the horrors of life all around? Our friend piled up heaps of injustice, war and destruction on the altar of perceived righteous indignation where he tends to sacrifice trust and belief.

My wife listened patiently and sought clarification. She described how her faith has allowed an invisible hand to steer her life towards the glory of grace, a gift she said she never imagined existed. Her gentleness swallowed the razor-sharp barbs of his intellectual prowess. Patience and kindness absorbed arrows aimed to pierce her devoted and loyal heart. The insistent attacks culminated in a preposterous challenge that in his mind would certainly prove his point beyond a shadow of doubt.

If her god really was the powerful, omniscient agent she claimed him to be, why did she not ask him for the time of day? My wife did not want to put the Lord to the test and did not know what to do. She felt she could only provoke her creator with such a request, and the challenge would have to go unanswered.

While our friend persevered in his demands, incited by the thrill of imminent victory, she prayed silently, fervently—if the Lord wanted to show his power she would not stand back. Deep down she sensed a divine whisper urging her on to ask for what he prepared her to hear.

"Two eighteen," she pronounced before she even got a chance to imagine what the correct time could be. They got out of the pool and peaked through the kitchen window beyond which the microwave's digital clock sent out a blazing crimson message penetrating the blackened air.

Two eighteen.

A chill traveled down her spine. She sought the warmth of the pool, shaken by the unexpected response and stunned by the answer she had feared would remain elusive.

His mind worked feverishly. He envisioned it had to have been between two and three o'clock. And under those circumstances, he believed, a one-in-sixty chance made a fluke, correct guess on her part not all too unlikely.

"You asked me," she said, "for that one thing over which I had no control, and God told you."

Our friend, I have not mentioned yet, is an adamant supporter of abortion rights. He repeatedly declares in public he will claim his entitlement to that procedure if one of his girlfriends slips up and conceives. Roe-versus-Wade gives him his marching orders. He may have never pondered his German home country's equivalent ruling. The right to terminate a perfectly healthy being is ciphered in the criminal code of law in paragraph…

Two eighteen.

My wife told this story to one of her friends who wondered out loud what God himself might have to say about that encounter. They opened the Scriptures, Matthew, the first gospel and book in the New Testament, and read about Jerusalem's cruel, outwitted Rome-enthroned king of the Jews.

In chapter two verse eighteen, "a voice is heard in Ramah, weeping and great mourning, Rachel weeping for her children and refusing to be comforted because they were no more."

Another friend of ours pointed out that in the Jewish faith the number 18 constitutes the sign of life. King Herod appears unimpressed as before.

I, the LORD, reveal myself to them in visions,
I speak to them in dreams.

NUMBERS 12:6

I'm probably not far off if I say you have heard, spoken or thought the following question: if God is both loving and all-powerful, why does he allow kids to have cancer, or something to that effect. No, I don't have quick and easy answers. But I have encountered situations that may shed at least a small light on this. Allow me to tell you about one such experience.

Twelve years ago my wife and I shared our faith in the Lord with our Jewish friend Mark Mogul, who has been a trusted colleague for over twenty-three years. He was kind and generous in his responses but made it clear that he did not share our belief. Five years later, he took care of one of my patients who fell ill while traveling to North Carolina where Mark worked at the time. After he gave me a clinical update on that patient on a Monday morning, he told me with great joy in his voice, "You are probably the first one who'd want to know. I got baptized yesterday." I'm not sure what was greater that moment, my elation or my surprise. What had happened, you might wonder?

God allowed him to have a few interesting experiences on his path to faith. His four-year-old son came home from his Jewish school one day and stated, "Dad, you know Jesus is God." Needless to say, his father reacted a bit perplexed. They don't teach that in orthodox Jewish schools. When Mark asked how he knew this, his son answered, "Come on Dad, everybody knows that." About a year later he asserted he had already met Jesus while "in Mommy's tummy."

Sometime later, one of Mark's patients shook up his world once again. Melanie, a beautiful five-year-old little girl, had been battling cancer for three and a half years and was dying of her disease. Mark and his colleagues had exhausted all treatment options and could do nothing more for her from a medical standpoint other than palliative care. For an entire week, Melanie reported a recurring dream. Each night two visitors came to see her. One was Jesus whom she recognized immediately. He told her he would take care of her and that she would be all right. As you can imagine, this brought great consolation to her mother. The second visitor was a five-year-old little boy. Melanie told her mom about him and explained that he scared her. Her mom gave a simple advice, "Just tell him to go away." In her dreams, Melanie did so, but nevertheless he returned every night. On the morning of her death she told her mom once again that he had appeared in her dream but this time he had introduced himself.

"My name is Salvatore," Melanie quoted the little boy. He said he had died of cancer four years earlier. "My father Sal works as a nurse on the pediatric cancer ward," she repeated his words. Surprisingly enough, Melanie did not know Sal had indeed lost a son named Salvatore who died from cancer. In his closing words, the little boy told Melanie, "You don't need to worry. Where you are going is amazing!"

Melanie's cancer and her spiritual journey impacted Mark in a dramatic way, though he was not the only one affected. Salvatore's father remained an avowed atheist until Melanie repeatedly encountered his son in the company of Jesus. Mark's and Sal's subsequent conversion and their walk with the Lord is a surprising yet stupendous result of this little girl's illness. As I keep on learning over and over again: God's ways are not our ways. You can listen to Mark's marvelous testimony if you google his name and Jesus.

Do you know where you are going?

Speak, Lord, for your servant is listening.
1 SAMUEL 3:9

For me, proof of the non-existence of nothingness was brief and to the point, and it came unexpectedly, from a child unaware of the controversy: a six-year old girl named Riley.

That day, Riley lay pale and listless in her bed. Her kidney tumor had recurred twice despite aggressive therapy. The hospital had exhausted all treatment options, and so she returned for the last time. Her father sat motionless and grim-faced; her brother sobbed. Riley's mother blotted her eyes and beamed an exuberant smile across the room that startled me to the core.

"I have to tell you a story," she said, as if nothing that transpired in the room mattered any more. "The other day, my husband and I sat talking in the living room, in the afternoon. Riley slept in her bedroom—at least we thought she was asleep. So it surprised us all the more when we heard her talking, because nobody else was visiting at the time. We couldn't understand a word she said, so we went over to see what was going on. She stood in the middle of her room and talked towards the ceiling in a language we've never heard before. I asked her, Riley, what are you doing? She continued to look up when she said, I'm talking to my Father."

Directing both arms towards her husband, the mother added, "I pointed at him and asked her, and who is this? Oh, that's my daddy, she said."

"Our Father who art in heaven. Hallowed be Thy Name. Thy kingdom come. Thy will be done, on earth as it is in heaven." In Riley's case, I have no doubt that his will found completion already here on earth.

I have often wondered which language Riley spoke that day. Neither she nor anyone in her extended family knew a foreign language or had even begun to learn one in school or elsewhere. Nor were they exposed to others who did.

Did that tongue represent the universal language our ancestors spoke before the days of the tower in Babel? Is there a heavenly language unrelated to all earthly dialects? I would love to listen, just to hear the sound of it, even though I might not comprehend a single word.

Not yet. Someday, though!

TWO

A BULLET DODGED

Everything is correct. Even the opposite.

Kurt Tucholsky

God heals, and the doctor takes the fee.

Benjamin Franklin

Needless to say, I hope you'll never be confronted with a cancer diagnosis in a loved one or in yourself. If you have gone through such an experience already, you likely remember the host of emotions that inundated you after you heard the terrible news. Pain, fear, frustration, anxiety, anger, nausea, numbness and sorrow may have all played a role.

These feelings may be so overwhelming that parents cannot focus on concrete steps to deal with this horrible challenge. When I look into a mother's or a father's eyes the first few moments after I have had to relay a cancer diagnosis, I believe I can see their stomachs drop.

Often enough, people tell me they are so in shock that they cannot speak or think coherently, or they state they do not know what to ask. But in due time the questions follow. What is it? What does it mean? Where do we go from here? These and many other questions usually have specific, concrete and occasionally even satisfactory answers. This is especially true in pediatrics where the majority of cancers are curable these days.

The one question oncologists struggle with the most is: Why? Why my child? Why now? Those are heart-wrenching questions. Some answers are simple and virtually always true, such as: I don't know. We simply know very little about why children get cancer. Other answers come to mind that are more complicated and perhaps should not be uttered at all because they may lack empathy or meaningfulness, and because they may not even be true. I have thought of, though not necessarily given answers like: Perhaps because your child can handle it better than some other kids can. Or: Perhaps you can handle it better than the next parent.

The one question I have learned to consider in this context, and sometimes talk about, is: Does suffering have a purpose? Having read the first chapter of this book, you may have already gotten a glimpse of an answer. As the stories of some of the children described in the coming chapters will tell, there is often a far bigger picture than what meets the eye at the first encounter.

If our God suffered and died, nailed to a wooden cross for our sake, would he not also remain involved, perhaps "behind the scene", at least in some instances? Would he not strengthen, lift up and correct by his own supernatural means what we as humans have managed to corrupt?

I cannot perceive some of the following cases as anything but divine intervention.

———————————

Eric was a shrimp. A munchkin. A little guy.

Small size, though, does not always equal frailty. Tough as leather, even at the tender age of eighteen months, he proved this fact in unsuspected ways.

Eric suffered from a brain tumor. Aggressive chemotherapy made adequate food intake nearly impossible for extended periods of time, and so one of our surgeons inserted a feeding tube directly through the abdominal wall into the stomach. That tube allowed nutritional support when Eric could not eat, and since he came to the hospital about every three weeks, he greatly benefited from this help.

Once again, Eric returned for yet another treatment, and things were going well.

Stephanie, who had recently graduated from nursing school, took care of him. For the first month of her employment she worked under the supervision of a more experienced nurse named Carissa. Carissa had been around forever, and she liked Stephanie and the way she handled herself.

"You want to go ahead and give Eric his meds? They are in the bin already," Carissa encouraged her protégé.

Stephanie nodded in delight. The more hands-on care she could provide, the more she liked working on the oncology ward. She found two syringes labeled with Eric's name and the prescribed medications. One contained a preparation to decrease the acid in his stomach. Another held a medicine to reduce nausea. A third syringe also carried Eric's name, but the sticker attached to it provided no additional information.

Injection of the first drug into the intravenous device implanted under the skin in Eric's chest went smoothly. The second went in equally well. The third, however, proved to be far more difficult. Stephanie knew a challenge when she saw one. She pushed hard, harder than ever before—but she was determined, and surrender was not an option.

"How is it going?" Carissa asked when she entered the room.

"Fine, really. I'm done with the first two. But this one, I don't know. This is hard."

Carissa peaked over Stephanie's shoulder. Three-fourths of the last medication had already found their way into Eric's bloodstream.

"What is that?" Carissa asked, unable to suppress a hint of suspicion.

"I don't know," Stephanie answered sheepishly.

"Let me see." Carissa disconnected the syringe. The remnant of the liquid with its odd, milky-yellow color did not look like any intravenous medications familiar to her. She brought the syringe to her nose.

"Smells like banana."

"What?" Stephanie panicked.

Carissa turned to Stephanie. "Mashed banana. You just gave him mashed banana IV instead of into the G-tube," she continued, pointing to the tube in his abdominal wall. Stephanie felt like throwing up.

Despite this horrible mistake with the potential for tragic consequences, Eric survived unharmed and unfazed.

Where in his body the intravenous mashed banana went remains obscure. We still wonder. To his lungs or his liver? To his brain? Or is it possible that God held his protective hands over him and supernaturally dealt with the problem? All I can say for sure is that Eric suffered no ill consequences at all.

Food for thought.

Little Eric required God's protection once for a human-made disaster. Olivia needed the Lord's safeguard not only once but on four separate occasions.

I met Olivia shortly after I came to my new hospital. She had been receiving treatment for leukemia since the age of four. Five months after her initial presentation, she should have been doing well, yet she complained of leg pain again, and her parents also noticed low-grade fevers. These symptoms were present when she first came to the hospital. Her mother voiced concerns for good reasons, although she knew that this disease rarely ever recurs so quickly.

A repeat bone marrow test established the presence of a type of leukemia that looked very different from that of the original diagnosis. Her ongoing treatment would never be effective for the newly discovered leukemia. Review of the original studies showed the old and the new findings to be virtually identical, and further examination confirmed that Olivia had been misdiagnosed. I was horrified. Looking back I realized that multiple people, including outside experts, were involved in the diagnosis, and I still don't fully understand what had happened. Hindsight, though, is always easy.

In any case, the "new" leukemia required much stronger therapy than the "old" one. No wonder Olivia ran into trouble.

Her prognosis was presumably still quite good because only a few months had elapsed. Present medical literature contains virtually no information on the outcome of therapy for misdiagnosed, inappropriately treated patients, and public acknowledgment of diagnostic mistakes on more than one occasion takes courage. Who wants to be an "expert" in that kind of medicine?

On an encouraging note, Olivia appeared to be the ultimate survivor. She certainly did not hesitate to voice her opinions and she came across as feisty. Those are the best prerequisites for a long life after a diagnosis of cancer, at least as far as children are concerned. She ran into trouble again only a few months later. Chapter two of her medical odyssey began almost delightfully.

Oftentimes, colorful pictures of tropical fish decorate modern treatment rooms in children's hospitals, or bright, vivid images of birds and flowers adorn the walls. This ambiance creates a short-lived, deceptive impression of a soothing, peaceful environment. Yet despite these efforts on our part, nothing but the notion of fear and pain comes to the minds of most children entering these places who quickly look through such ruses, no matter their age. It takes them seconds to discover the true purpose of these rooms, which serve as a place for painful medical procedures.

Olivia lay comfortably on the examination stretcher. She was all too familiar with her "child-friendly" surroundings. The thought of the procedure she faced, however, did not bother her much. Still, her attitude was the exception and not the rule.

"Roll over on your side and look towards your mom," Dr. Lewis said. "Good, now cuddle up."

Olivia knew exactly what the doctor wanted her to do. "Like a kitty-cat?" she asked her.

"Like a kitty-cat. You know all the tricks, don't you?" Dr. Lewis replied, smiling.

"Yep."

"Who taught you?"

"You did."

"Is that why you always lie so still?" she asked.

Olivia did not answer. She was busy scratching her nose. The medication one of the two nurses in the room had injected moments earlier did not only distract and relax her—invariably, it also made her nose itch.

Dr. Lewis glanced over her shoulder. "Did you check the chemo?" she asked the other nurse behind her.

"Yeah, I did. It's hers. Nobody else is getting a spinal today," the nurse answered.

People considered Carla one of the most experienced nurses on the cancer ward, and one of the best.

Dr. Lewis examined the syringe Carla showed her. It contained the translucent, yellow fluid she expected. Olivia's name and the name of the medication, Methotrexate, were clearly printed on the label.

They transferred the medicine into a second, sterile syringe. Dr. Lewis took a mere twenty seconds to inject the fluid into the spinal canal of her small patient who lay curled up so quietly in front of her.

Olivia did not feel a thing. Dr. Lewis could perform the procedure in her sleep if need be. She had performed it on a thousand occasions. A few minutes later, Olivia lay back in her room where she slept for half an hour until new-found energy brought her back on her feet.

Judging by her appearance, no one could have known that anything ever went wrong with Olivia—quite the contrary. Her mother usually suffered exhaustion in just trying to keep up with her daughter! Olivia could not sit still, and following instructions did not constitute part of her vocabulary. And her father wanted a second child, much to her mother's chagrin. He hardly ever interacted with his daughter before dinner time. By that point, Olivia finally ran out of steam—as did her mother. It brought her mother great relief, as far as the treatment was concerned, that things were finally running smoothly for a change.

An hour and a half before the end of her shift, Carla looked forward to a quiet evening, but she knew there was work left to be done before she could sign out to the colleague scheduled to replace her. She still needed to hang Olivia's intravenous chemotherapy, so she headed to the refrigerator behind the nurses' station, which contained all the medications the pharmacy staff had prepared for that afternoon.

Carla found the correct syringe immediately because only this particular one displayed the appropriate yellow color. The other syringes in the medication bin contained clear or red fluid. The syringe carried Olivia's name and the name of the correct medication.

And it bore the letters "IT", indicating its purpose, namely the injection into Olivia's spinal fluid.

Carla frowned, and then her stomach dropped. Olivia had already received her spinal chemotherapy shortly before lunch. Carla had handed the syringe to Dr. Lewis herself. Carla ran back to the treatment room and began frantically inverting and shaking the plastic disposal container full of discarded needles and syringes, ripping off with brute force the safety device on the top so she could spill its contents on the floor.

"What are you doing?" Betty, the charge nurse, asked in dismay. Carla's behavior had never alarmed her before.

"I'm looking for a syringe."

"Why?"

Carla did not respond.

"Be careful," Betty admonished her, "don't stick yourself. Watch out for those needles."

"I don't care."

"Calm down. What on earth is going on?"

Carla did not reply. She handed Betty the full syringe instead. "Here."

Betty read the label. "Didn't Olivia have her spinal this morning?" she asked, taken aback.

"Eleven thirty."

"Oh my god."

Carla found the other, empty syringe and handed it to Betty. On the label were printed Olivia's name and the name of the correct medicine. And it said "IV", for intravenous infusion, with the appropriate dose as well. Olivia had received the correct medicine, but at a dose of one hundred and thirty milligrams, which was more than ten times higher than it should have been.

Distraught and nauseated, Carla informed Olivia's mother. Olivia did not participate in their conversation and did not bother to listen either. She felt fine, and things more important came to her mind. Before the sedative and pain medications from that morning had worn off, she had slept for a while and now the limits of her energy knew no bounds.

I served as the on-call physician that night. Betty phoned and reported the calamitous incident. She volunteered no excuses and did not know what to do. Carla, she said, sat devastated in the nurses' lounge.

I could not help but laugh.

Now, you must not think I found this occurrence particularly amusing, or that I had any interest in seeing Olivia suffer injury from such an unfortunate mistake. We had reason enough to worry about her. Serious and permanent brain damage, even death, can result from an incorrect or too much of a suitable medication given into the spinal canal. The safe amounts of medications for injection into the spine have long been established and published in the medical literature. By all accounts, Olivia had received more medicine than she ever should have. Much more.

I could not push Carla's emotional turmoil aside. She suffered because she felt responsible and could do nothing to reverse the unfortunate incident. In truth, she did not carry the entire responsibility. The physician always bears the primary responsibility for his or her actions. Dr. Lewis injected the wrong medicine, not Carla. Dr. Lewis had the obligation to check the label prior to giving the medicine and to read all the information provided, but she had not yet become aware of the mistake.

No, I laughed because of a surreal—and suddenly quite relevant—decades-old story of another young leukemia patient. When I first heard this story a few weeks earlier, I did not realize it would come in handy so soon.

While visiting my family in Germany, I took a leisurely afternoon stroll across the hills to the local children's hospital nestled in the woods. The senior pediatric cancer specialist there had announced his retirement within another month. A blurb in the local newspaper had aroused my curiosity, and I wanted to see how his work differed from our medical practice in the United States.

A secretary walked me into a large office full of books and scientific journals. The retiring colleague, a friendly old man, got up from behind his desk to shake my hand. His white hair matched a stiffly-starched, formal lab coat, but his eyes shone young and curious. He clearly loved what he had devoted himself to for a lifetime.

"Where did you train?" he asked after I described my work in Florida.

"Seattle," I replied, and thinking he might not know that city, I added, "in Washington State". Europeans often have no idea that the capital city and also a state far away carry the same name. In the late sixties, a transplant physician now renowned for his research and discoveries moved from the old world to Seattle. Disembarking his plane, he still thought he had reached a D.C. suburb rather than a location three thousand miles across the continent in the Pacific Northwest—though not for long. To his amazement, he saw mountains beyond any expectation. Moreover, he could not find the capital's monuments he so admired on photos. Nevertheless, he soon fell in love with the place and remains there to this day.

But my German colleague knew Seattle.

"Is Archie Bleyer still there?" The name of an American oncologist on his lips surprised me. Archie Bleyer, known as "Mr. Methotrexate", proved instrumental in working out the appropriate spinal doses of that medication.

"I briefly met him when he was still in Seattle, but he moved to Houston a few years ago," I answered.

"I called Archie once. Must have been at least twenty years ago," he continued, scratching his chin. "I read one of his papers on Methotrexate and spinal therapy. Until these publications came out, we didn't really know what the safe doses were. Back then, everybody did whatever he thought might be right. I know this must sound awful to you now, but it's the truth. I told him my story. I took care of a leukemia patient, in the days prior to those fancy IVs. All his veins had collapsed. I held the chemo, Methotrexate, in my hand, about a hundred and thirty milligrams, but I didn't know what to do. In desperation, I gave it all into the kid's spinal canal."

"All one hundred and thirty?"

"Yes!"

Such a story had never crossed my radar screen.

"What happened?"

"Nothing. Well, that's not true. He developed no problems but he went into a full remission. After that, I gave a hundred milligrams to the big kids, and fifty to the smaller ones. I never encountered any problems."

"That's hard to believe."

To put this in perspective, fifteen milligrams is the safe dose for adults and adolescents. Lower doses are appropriate for younger children.

"What did Archie say?"

"He thought this was very interesting, but he suggested I stick to the lower doses. Turns out they are as effective as the higher doses, as you know yourself. He said I should publish my data," he added.

"Did you?"

"Yes, a long time ago. You want a copy? Let's see what I did with that paper." He rummaged through his files and retrieved a reprint of his publication. "You know, I spent a year in America myself. Minnesota. I applied for a position there in Minneapolis, but they rejected me. I had pretty much resigned myself to the fact when the program director called two or three months later and offered me the position. One of the other interns got fired. He was great actually—kind of." A big smirk spread over his face.

"What do you mean?" "Great" and "fired" sounded suspiciously contradictory. The story had to have a fishy ending.

"No one in the whole hospital could draw blood faster than this guy. In those days, hospitals did not employ phlebotomists. Every morning, we ran around and obtained blood from our patients ourselves. It took me an hour, at least. Well, this guy was the fastest gun for hire, so to speak. All of us envied him until one morning one of the nurses walked in on him as he drew blood from a young girl. He stuck her with a long needle right into the heart." He spread his thumb and index finger wide apart to indicate the grotesque length of the needle. Then he formed a fist and, with a swift gesture, pretended to stab his own chest as if he wanted to give more weight to the incident by recreating it in front of my eyes.

"I guess he didn't get to stay much longer after that, did he?"

"You got that right. He left in a heartbeat," he laughed, "no pun intended. That's how I got my chance."

I walked home enriched by a gorgeous afternoon in the hills, wondering why none of my colleague's patients ever developed problems despite the apparent ten-fold overdoses of a powerful, poisonous medication. I remember thinking I had learned two great stories with little practical purpose. In our practice, no one ever received more than fifteen milligrams, even the biggest adolescents and young adults.

Betty's call brought these memories back in a flash. Driving to the hospital to examine Olivia and talk to her parents, I knew by sharing this experience I might make them feel a bit better. In addition, I might provide a few other people with a chance to take a deep breath of relief.

At seven o'clock, Olivia still ran hard and strong in her room. Her mother, in contrast, paced the halls. She was scared and shaking. I felt sorry for her because she and her daughter had already gone through so much.

I reiterated the obvious mistake she already knew about, the doses involved and the potential dangers. The story from Germany gave her consolation that things might turn out all right. I drained as much spinal fluid and with it as much medicine from Olivia's back as was feasible and prescribed a decent dose of steroids to reduce any ensuing inflammation in the brain. I told her mother I would come back in the morning and repeat the procedure.

Olivia did not suffer any harm. We expected headaches, seizures, nerve damage, memory problems, but she developed none of them.

Chapter three of this horrific saga commenced a few months later, after Olivia returned to the hospital one afternoon for another round of chemotherapy. This time, she shared a double room with another patient named Charley. He lay in the bed next to Olivia's. Charley carried the diagnosis of medulloblastoma, which is a common form of a brain tumor, and he required treatment as well.

In the middle of the afternoon, Charley's nurse Dawn checked the refrigerator with the chemotherapy drugs for the third time. As on the prior two occasions, she found none of the medications the doctor had ordered for Charley, so she called the pharmacy in exasperation and complained to the staff technician. Considering Charley's admission in the morning, his treatment should have begun a long time ago.

The technician phoned back a few moments later. One of her colleagues had delivered the medications in question hours ago.

In the interim, Olivia's treatment went well. She showed no side effects and lay comfortably in bed 9B. Her nurse, Gabriella, was beside herself and could not finish her shift when Dawn discovered what had happened. Somehow, Gabriella had confused the kids' charts and the respective instructions. The chemotherapy orders were intended for Charley who slouched in bed 9A. By the time Dawn detected the mistake, the infusion of these medicines was long complete.

How much more could go wrong for this little girl? Why did these things always happen to her? Looking back over more than twenty-eight years, I am not aware of another patient who underwent therapy for a misdiagnosed illness or received someone else's medication or an overdose of chemotherapy. To the team's and the hospital's defense, if any exists, we made more mistakes with Olivia than with all other patients in our care in those years combined. The hospital worked hard to implement strategies and procedures to minimize such occurrences. Modern computer technology promises to help prevent the "human error." Olivia may have done well because of the drugs we gave her inadvertently. Perhaps she was destined to do well with any therapy and could have brushed off cyanide. Who knows?

It may be difficult to fathom, but Olivia was still not safe from her doctors and nurses. Not more than two months later, she came back to the clinic, where her favorite nurse hooked her up to an IV pole. Chemotherapy dripped into her intravenous device in her chest. But instead of resting in the treatment room where she should have been in the first place, she stood in the hall, chatting with the nurses. She leaned against the counter of the nurses' station while the pole stood five feet to the side, the clear IV tubing dangling in between the two. Another nurse in a rush did not see the tubing, ran right into it and ripped the access needle out of Olivia's chest. One scream followed another, blood splattered, the chemotherapy fluid ran on the floor and mayhem ensued. Again, as on the prior three occasions, Olivia did surprisingly well, the momentary shock notwithstanding.

If we had difficulty finding a nurse to take care of Olivia voluntarily before this last occurrence, it took a heavy bribe or worse to identify one afterwards. I'm not sure how Olivia got *any* therapy after this last incident. Who in his right mind wants to pilot a cursed plane?

For sure, I do not want to investigate the medicines she received in the final months of her therapy. Better not to open a can of worms.

Wait, this is not the end of the story. There is, after all, an epilogue. Fast forward many, many years. One of our patients, another little girl with leukemia and her mother were shopping at a local store when a stranger approached them in one of the aisles. She had noticed the girl's bald head and drawn the correct conclusion that chemotherapy was the most likely culprit. The stranger, you may have already guessed, was Olivia's mother.

She said I had saved her daughter's life. I'm grateful for the kind words, but she's not correct. All *I* ever really did was remember an old story. *God* saved her life. He knew what he was doing back then. He always does. He wanted Olivia to work for him one day, and this day has come. Olivia, I hear, is "some kind of a pastor".

So Olivia is doing God's work now? The "why" question is coming back full force. Why was Olivia the one for whom everything went wrong? By no means do I want to diminish our responsibility in her misdiagnosis and mistreatment on several occasions. But allow me to ask this question: Could there have been a bigger picture? A spiritual warfare scenario, where someone tried to foil the Lord's plans at all cost? Someday I hope to be able to ask him that question.

The Lord says he won't burden us with more than we can handle—but occasionally he does crank up the heat to see how faithful we are in our relationship with him. Sometimes, though, we only misinterpret the load God asks us to carry.

Marshall suffered from sickle cell anemia. He lived with his grandmother who treated the risks of infection in this dreadful disease with utmost respect. Marshall returned from school earlier than expected one day, complaining of a headache and aches and pains in his legs. Suspicious of his symptoms and noticing that he felt very warm, she took him straight to the emergency room. The nurse in the triage area asked her why Marshall had come to the hospital.

"He's got a fever," she said, shortening the story to one of its essential ingredients.

"How high did it get?"

"Three-hundred and fifty."

The nurse pulled herself together and continued with as much calm as she could muster, "How did you know it had climbed up that high?"

"Cause I been cookin' in the kitchen all day. I touched the stove and then I touched his forehead, and it was about the same."

Grandma proved correct. He did have fever after all, though a bit lower than the one she reported. We kept him for two days, just to make sure it did not get up that high again.

———————————

One should never underestimate the wit, intelligence and feistiness the Lord plants and nurtures in the children involved in our lives. But I catch myself doing just that—often too late—all the time. A few years ago, I encountered a patient whom I had not seen for several years after she had completed her therapy for her muscle tumor. When I asked her whether she remembered me at all, she gave me a stern look and, with as deep a voice as she could bring forth, she replied, "Yeah, you called me rawhide". I intended that to convey my sense of admiration for her resilience back then, but I had forgotten I had ever said that to her. Apparently, she had not!

Yvonne is a case in point. She had a history of infant leukemia, a highly aggressive blood cancer. At two-and-a-half years of age, she had completed her therapy. I could not remember our last encounter—it must have been several months earlier—when she came to the clinic for follow-up purposes. She stood in the reception hall by herself while her mother talked to a staff member around the corner.

"Yvonne, you've grown so much!" I exclaimed.

I swear I intended that comment as a compliment, but Yvonne gave me a dirty look. "Yeah, and I'm not done yet," she scolded me and set me straight!

———————————

Author, flutist, and neuroblastoma survivor. These attributes come to mind when I think of Annette. She's also a quiet and reserved munchkin. One day she came back in the hospital for routine chemotherapy and she was tolerating everything well. I tried to get her to come out of her shell but I had little success. She didn't laugh when I told a joke; she didn't respond to a short story of another patient; and she rolled her eyes when I tickled her foot.

Annette couldn't have cared less. With indifference she asked, "Don't you have any other patients to take care of?"

Smarty pants!

———————————

The last time I heard from Eric, Olivia, Marshall, Yvonne and Annette or their respective families, I learned that they were doing well. Why do I write about them? All of them faced tremendous challenges, and despite their young age they persevered magnificently. In their victories, small and large, they give us encouragement to deal with life's difficulties and set-backs.

There is a second reason. In the minds and faces of these children, I see a part of God himself. After all, he tells us that he created us in his image. To be a part of children's lives, and to learn from and grow with them, is a great privilege. In our interactions with them, we get to learn more about ourselves. We may even get to meet God through them. It happened to me.

THREE

HARK! THE HERALD ANGELS

To die: to sleep; to sleep: perchance to dream;
Aye, there's the rub

WILLIAM SHAKESPEARE, HAMLET

The creative human mind has invented a long list of modern devices that allow us to communicate with one another at any time and at any location. Even at the ends of the world, cell phones and computers provide instant connection. Let us not forget, however, that God has at his disposal one vehicle of interaction with his creation that is never available at humanity's beck and call. Angels have met with and talked to humans at least since early biblical times. They are God's messengers to his people. Moses and the writers of the New Testament Gospels documented their experiences and encounters with the host of heaven long ago. Despite evidence in the biblical literature, common objections dictate that angels are figments of our fevered imagination. If they genuinely exist in the heavenly realms and in the earthly world, no matter how sporadic their appearances might be, then we should not be surprised to find conclusive evidence of their presence here among us.

According to an old German proverb, children and drunkards tell the truth. Sometimes we are blessed to meet children who prove this claim correct

———————————

In the New Testament Book of Acts, Luke tells an amazing story. Herod, the king of Israel, has incarcerated the apostle Peter. In the night before his trial, a voice only Peter can hear wakes him up. *"Suddenly an angel of the Lord appeared,"* Luke writes. *"Quick, get up,"* the angel tells Peter, and shortly thereafter, he adds this command: *"Follow me."* It is hard to imagine one could refuse to obey an angel.

Nine-year-old Ronald was a delightful and outgoing young man who suffered from a hideous and destructive brain tumor. Multiple rounds of chemotherapy, surgery and radiation treatments over a two-year span caused pain and agony but did not prevent a recurrence of the cancer.

His parents naturally wanted everything done. They insisted on heroic measures, including chest compressions and a breathing machine, should his condition deteriorate to the point that he could no longer sustain life himself, regardless of whether such actions only prolonged his suffering. Unfortunately, as far as reasonable therapies were concerned, everything had already been done. Often enough in cancer therapy everything is far too insufficient.

Ronald always looked the picture of good health. His skin revealed a nice pink color. His heart beat with the steadiness of a Swiss clock, yet death stood but a breath away.

"Ronald, open your eyes," I whispered in his ear. He did not budge to indicate he heard, let alone understood. His pupils reacted sluggishly to the beam of a flashlight. A pinch on the bottom of his foot should have been painful enough for him to withdraw his leg, but he did not move.

"Any idea how much longer?" I quietly asked the nurses.

The nurse on the other side of the bed who prepared an intravenous infusion shrugged her shoulders. She did not know and neither did anyone else. Soon, it had to be soon. Day after day, I entered the intensive care unit, expecting Ronald to have died the prior night, and every morning he had survived yet another twenty-four hours.

"We don't want him to die in the intensive care unit," his mother said suddenly. This statement reflected an unexpected and remarkable change in the parents' desire for intervention. "It's not that they don't give good care here. Please don't misunderstand. It's that we've always been upstairs. All the nurses there on the ward know him."

I nodded in assent. For weeks we had been hoping that Ronald might experience a peaceful death. Nobody wanted to prolong his dying and have him suffer from accelerated but futile medical care.

His body remained flaccid on the way back to the cancer ward and his eyes stayed closed. Gone were the days he could respond to his environment. The tumor robbed him of himself. It stole from him the essence of his humanity. No longer would he be able to say his good-byes, but if nothing else, at least he could die in his parents' arms. They would forever cherish that experience, difficult as it promised to be.

The nurses lifted Ronald's fragile, limp body onto his new bed. He lay motionless for the next few hours, while his mother sat on a chair next to his bed.

All of a sudden Ronald raised his head and propped up his trunk on his elbow.

"Mom" he said with the clearest of voices, "the angels are coming for me now." When he sank down on his pillow, the angels took him with them.

During his banishment on the island of Patmos, the apostle John is generally believed to have written the Book of Revelation after he experienced a series of visions. One of these visions in particular has stuck with me. I have long cherished discovering rainbows in the sky, ever since Mike used the rainbow the Lord sent him to ascend into heaven. *Then I saw another mighty angel coming down from heaven,"* John writes. *"He was robed in a cloud, with a rainbow above his head."* What a gripping image. Who gets to travel in the sky on a cloud?

Lindsey was 8 years old and suffered from a tumor of her chest wall. One night, her father called. "Hi, Doc, this is Lindsey's father. How are you doing?"

"Fine, thanks. What's going on?"

"Lindsey has been having trouble with her stomach."

"What kind of trouble? Pain?"

"No, not real…delta two thirty five…"

"What?" I was not sure I had heard correctly.

"…turn left heading two one zero join one eight left localizer. I think it's more like cramps. She feels hungry and eats, and a short time later she feels a lot of pressure."

"Any vomiting, diarrhea or constipation?"

"No. She went to the bathroom twice today and once yester…delta two thirty five you are…"

"Excuse me?"

"…cleared for ILS one eight left approach. I think she's all right as far as that goes."

"Are you talking to me?" I wasn't sure what was going on.

"Yes, sorry," he apologized.

"Does she have any fevers or breathing problems?"

"No fevers. And she's breathing fine. You think she could have an ulcer?"

"Sure, that's possible."

"What do you do for that?"

"Well, first we have to figure out what it is. She may need to see a stomach doctor. They may want to look inside her stomach and do a few biopsies."

"How soon do you think we should do that? If we bring her delta two thirty five contact Newberg tower one one niner point five..."

"What?"

"...you are cleared to land runway one eight left. If we bring her tomorrow morning..."

He was obviously not just communicating with me.

"I'm sorry but who are you talking to all this time?" I asked.

"Just a pilot."

"A pilot?"

"Yeah, I'm landing a plane."

"You don't want to hang up and call me when you're done?"

"No, that's all right."

"You're sure?"

"We're OK, he's on the ground. So what about tomorrow, can you see her?"

"I think that would be a *good* idea." I did not want him to continue the conversation while he was landing a plane full of hundreds of people.

"Do I have to make an appointment?"

"No, no, that's fine. Take care of your planes and come between nine and eleven, OK?"

"Great, thanks, Doc."

Lindsey and her parents came the next morning. All of the planes had apparently made it back safely onto solid ground. Pressure over Lindsey's stomach made her uncomfortable, but she felt better already. An acid blocker alleviated her symptoms, allowing her to continue chemotherapy.

A year and a half after the end of her therapy, Lindsey returned with bone pain and fevers. Further studies showed that a bone marrow cancer reared its ugly head, presumably as the result of her prior chemotherapy. Not even a marrow transplant could cure her new disease, despite the fact that we were able to find a perfect donor for her quite quickly. Her parents were devastated.

A few weeks before she passed away, Lindsey lay in her bed. Her parents and her brother checked on her and found her with a peaceful smile. She had lost a lot of weight and looked very weak.

"How are you, sweetheart? Any pain?" her father asked her.

"It's OK."

"You want one of your pain pills?"

"No, not now."

"I noticed you were smiling when we came into the room. What were you thinking about?" her mother asked.

Lindsey sat up straight in her bed. "I went up there with my angel," she countered, pointing to the ceiling.

"With your angel? Where?"

"Up into the sky."

"How?"

"He came on a cloud, for *me!*"

"That was a dream?"

"No, I wasn't sleeping."

"What did you do?" her brother wanted to know.

"We flew everywhere. It was so white. There was so much light. He took me everywhere."

"What did he look like?"

"I don't know. White. All white."

Lindsey's father brought planes safely and skillfully up into and down from the sky. He found consolation in the fact that someone else, more qualified than he could ever be, stepped in to take care of his daughter from then on. On her heaven-bound flight, Lindsey traveled with an air controller of her very own.

A few years ago, I read the Koran. In light of all the political turmoil in the world and the religious fervor heating up all around us, I thought I ought to try to understand where people with an entirely different spiritual background come from. One "Sure", or chapter of the Koran, contains a claim that I have never forgotten. "God chooses messengers from among the angels and from among the men; surely God is Hearing, Seeing," it says.

I realize this is not a biblical truth, but still I wonder whether it holds legitimacy. If God indeed picks and chooses from among men, at least under some circumstances, what would that look like?

I believe I got at least one answer when a colleague of mine, with whom I shared the story above, told me about a girl in his care.

Amy lay asleep in her bed late in the afternoon. Her mother sat by her side. She was no longer willing to leave her daughter alone under any circumstance. She did not expect Amy to survive beyond a few days, although the doctor had refused for months to pinpoint a date. He mentioned to her once how often he was wrong later on when he predicted the life expectancy of his terminally ill patients. Even if he could have been certain—and pride often pushed him to presume such certainty—he would not have wanted to say it aloud.

"All you'd do is waiting for that time, for that day to come. It'd be cruel. You need to lead your life with Amy as if every new day's the last one you have with her," he had said.

During the final clinic visit, she asked the doctor again, not expecting an answer. He responded in a manner more concrete than ever before. "Days, a few weeks," he replied in the hallway where Amy could not overhear them. Her mother was shocked, although she knew intuitively simply by looking at her daughter. For weeks she had imagined it would end like this, and yet when the time came, that recognition devastated her.

Amy's weak and frail body seemed like it would break in half, were she to step out of bed. Her lymphoma and the chemotherapy she had received for years rendered her bones brittle and vulnerable; they would snap, her mother feared, if Amy bore weight on them. With tears in her eyes she looked out of the window to the pine trees in their back yard.

"Don't cry mom," Amy pleaded when she woke up.

Her mother stroked Amy's spindly thin arm. "I'm sorry, Honey. It's …" She swallowed hard and could barely finish the sentence, "I'm going to miss you so much."

"I'll miss you, too, Mom. And Dad…But I'll be all right," she added with a sudden smile.

"I know you'll be fine," her mother replied, pointing upward with one finger.

"No, I already met my angel."

"*Your* angel? What do you mean?" she asked. She didn't know anybody had a personal angel.

"A real angel. She's *my* angel."

"She?"

"Yeah, it's a she. She's wonderful." Amy possessed her mother's full attention. "Can you tell me more about her?"

Amy thought for a moment. "She talked to me," she said.

"About what?"

"Oh, everything."

"When did you meet her?"

"A while ago. She said I'd meet her again soon."

"I wish I could meet her, too."

"You'd like her a lot, Mom."

"Anything else you remember?"

Amy hesitated.

"No… I don't know…Oh yes, her name is Abigail."

Amy never mentioned her angel again. She passed away in the presence of her parents a few days later. Whenever her mother looked skyward, she wondered what Amy and her angel were up to in heaven, wherever exactly that was. Friends, family and people she barely knew told her for months that things would get better, that the pain would ease and that time would spread a veil of mercy and forgetfulness over her suffering. Well intended though they were, these comments only made matters worse. The memory of Amy often sent a stabbing pain through her mother's chest that lost none of the first few days' intensity.

Nine months after Amy's death, her mother sat on a park bench on the playground where she had taken Amy the first few years of her short but precious life. Spring had chased away the dread of winter. Trees and shrubs stood in full bloom while children played in the sand and on the swings and slides. Seeing the little ones hurt her, yet for reasons not entirely clear to her, she came back to the same place. Over and over, she returned.

"Why do you go if it hurts you so much," her husband once asked her.

"I don't know," she answered before she added, almost whispered, "If I don't go, it hurts even more."

People rested on the other benches around the playground, but she sat by herself on her bench. An older woman approached. "May I sit down?" she asked politely.

"Sure, please. There's plenty room for both of us."

"Thank you."

A moment of silence ensued.

"It's wonderful to see those kids, isn't it?" the older woman questioned. Amy's mother did not answer. Tears rolling down her cheeks, she pulled out a handkerchief and noisily blew her nose.

"I'm sorry," she apologized.

"No, no. It's all right. I hope I didn't…I didn't mean to…"

"You didn't…it's me." Disquieted, they avoided eye contact altogether.

"I love kids, too," Amy's mother replied after she regained her composure.

The older woman nodded. "You have any?"

"Used to. Not anymore. …I had a daughter. She passed away last year. Cancer, lymphoma."

"I'm so sorry."

"Thanks. She's up there in heaven." She gestured with her head toward the sky. Cumulus clouds drifted overhead while two minutes of silence passed.

"I know how you feel," the older woman said, looking over her shoulder.

"How can you?" Amy's mother countered, her response harsher than she intended. The other woman ignored the slight and replied quietly, "I had a daughter once, too."

Amy's mother, who had focused on a tree in the distance, turned to her. "You did?"

"It's been a long time. The hurt never went away, even after all those years."

Amy's mother faced the playground again as the other added softly, "I loved my Abigail so much."

———————

One of the worst rebels in my professional life also turned out to be one of the nicest, most engaging young people I ever dealt with. Rebels rarely listen to human warning and lay down their arms. A supernatural voice, in contrast, may elicit an entirely different response. Deep in Shemot, the second book of the Jewish Scriptures known by Christians as Exodus, the Lord gives us an explicit warning and an invitation at the same time. Moses writes almost thirty-four hundred years ago, "*See, I am sending an angel ahead of you to guard you along the way and to bring you to the place I have prepared. Pay attention to him and listen to what he says. Do not rebel against him.*" I want to tell you about my rebel who finally ceased his insurrection. Admittedly, I miss his playful mutiny very much.

In hindsight, the first ambush should have been warning enough. I had no excuses falling into a similar trap a second time. The third time, I looked like a fool.

I walked into Todd's room one morning, ready to start a new day. Pulling back the curtain to begin my examination, I expected Todd to be asleep because it was very quiet. A splatter of water from a large syringe hit me squarely in the chest and awoke me rudely out of my morning stupor. Anger welled up within me momentarily but then I could not help but share in Todd's laughter. Todd was too nice a kid for me to hold his prank against him.

Three weeks later, the initial assault long forgotten, I once again entered a darkened room where I naively anticipated Todd sound asleep. Instead, his mischievous hand reached around the curtain and showered me with layers of silly string, which stuck to my hair, my clothes and my stethoscope. It took me five minutes to clean it all off, and I swore I would never make the same mistake again.

Two weeks after this last incident, payback time was at hand. I snuck into the dimly-lit room without a sound, planning to pin him in his bed and tickle every last bone in his body. Complete silence would have reigned if not for Todd's deep, rhythmic breath sounds.

Kreeek, Krirk. The awful sound of glass or similar material crushed under my feet stopped me dead in my tracks. Laughter from behind the curtain told me all I needed to know. Todd had spread little packages of explosives throughout the front of his room. The place turned out to be a veritable minefield designed to trap me before I could ever come close enough for revenge.

Todd brimmed with creativity and imagination, and he possessed a great sense of humor to boast. At twelve years of age, he should have been spending his time with friends and family rather than in a hospital with medical people, fighting a vicious tumor of the adrenal gland. When he stopped playing tricks, we knew his disease had returned. His wasted, pale body signaled that he would not survive much longer, and I knew telling him so was surely the most difficult task his parents had ever faced.

A few days later, I found Todd lying on his bed, clutching a small, black travel bag tightly to his side. I would have given much for another surprise attack. His face exuded tranquility.

"I'm ready," he said with a serene smile.

I nodded. "What's that?" I asked, pointing to the bag.

"Oh, my favorite CDs and a couple of books. My favorite stuff. I'll take 'em with me."

"You think they'll let you play your music up there in heaven?"

"Of course." Todd already knew the music he would hear.

Later, Todd pointed to the foot end of his bed. His father noticed Todd in a trance.

"What are you looking at?" he questioned.

"There's an angel sitting on my bed," Todd answered as if that was the most natural thing in the world. Our rebel's mutiny came to a close. From now on, he responded to a different calling. He passed away peacefully.

His parents buried Todd's travel bag with him. They imagine Todd hears music in heaven even without his CDs.

Karl Barth, the Swiss theologian, once wrote that the angels play Mozart to entertain themselves but Bach to delight God. Todd, I fear, has more rambunctious music in mind. *He's a rebel* by The Crystals or David Bowie's *Rebel rebel* would fit him a lot better.

––––––––––

In the Book of Acts, Luke tells us an incredibly sad story. A righteous man named Stephen is falsely accused, wrongly condemned and ultimately stoned to death. And yet it is, at its heart, a beautiful story. For when Stephen sees heaven open, he asks for forgiveness for those committing their injustice against him, even in the moment of his death. His accusers, Luke writes, "*saw that his face was like the face of an angel.*" How did they know this? Had they seen angels? Were they familiar with such appearances? And if he *did* look like an angel, why did they not act more carefully in their condemnation and why did they not hesitate in procuring false witnesses against him? That brings up the question: if humans look like angels, or vice versa, how would we know?

Brian and I talked on the phone three times before we met in person. Based on his voice, my mind created the picture of an intense, obsessed older man. A highly aggressive brain tumor affected Brian's fourteen-year old son, and after multiple therapies in various institutions around the country had failed, Norm's death appeared imminent. Brian had heard of an unusual case with promising investigational treatment at our hospital and wanted to pursue it for his son.

I hesitated. The desperation in Brian's voice on the phone suggested unrealistic expectations, and long-distance travel to yet another hospital and an entirely unfamiliar environment could not be in Norm's best interest. The family lived in a small town close to the Georgia border. Brian would have none of it. He had made up his mind; he and Norm insisted on coming to our hospital.

A week later, a robust, resolute younger man with only one arm came into the office. For a brief moment I stood confused. Norm had a brain tumor, not an amputated arm. The scenario made sense when a second individual walked in behind the first. *He*, in turn, did have the unsteady gait of a patient with a tumor in the back of the brain, and the sparse radiation-burned hair.

The father introduced himself as Brian. I was immediately struck by how much he smiled despite the horrible ordeal he and his son were going through. He exemplified joy and the embodiment of hope, despite the sad story he related. Nobody in Brian's family appeared shocked when he developed bone cancer at a young age, although the fact that he survived thirty years later impressed them as extraordinary. Cancer struck at least four children or young adults not only in his but also in each of the preceding two generations. A genetic defect as yet unidentified had to be responsible for the many individuals with cancer in Brian's family.

Norm himself, as it turned out, not Brian, had decided to pursue one more round of increasingly experimental treatments. After all, Norm possessed his father's genes—not only the cruel cancer gene but also the amplified gene of life and hope. "I'll try one more time," Norm said with slurred speech but a disarming smile.

Upon his return a few weeks later, the tumor showed obvious signs of progression. Norm could barely speak, and his gait appeared visibly worse. Although he soon drifted into unconsciousness, his parents remained grateful for all the caregivers in their lives and the extra time they had been given. They had tried everything, and they had not failed their son.

Two days before Norm passed away, Brian reported a conversation when Norm could still interact coherently. We sat face to face, and Brian told me in great detail the course of that interaction:

Norm had woken up from a dream, apparently a wonderful dream, but he could not remember any details. Brian sat with him and waited patiently.

"Nothing you recall?" he asked after a while. "Where were you?"

"I don't know."

"What were you doing?"

"I don't remember."

"Well, maybe you'll remember later. You want lunch?" he changed the subject, thinking he would not get anywhere with his questions.

"No, wait!" Urgency rang from Norm's voice. He moved his head back and forth as if he wanted to shake his memories free from the matrix of his brain where they got stuck.

"Is it coming back now?" his dad asked.

"I saw an older man."

"Somebody you know?"

"I don't think so."

He looked out of the window, expecting the answer in the cloudless northern Florida sky. With his memory returning ever so slowly, he described an unusual encounter. The man he portrayed was shockingly familiar to his parents, but they did not tell him so. Norm, they were convinced, had seen his grandfather who died of a heart condition during Norm's infancy.

"Did he talk to you?" Brian asked him.

"I don't know."

"Did he do something with you, or for you?" Brian would not let up.

"No, he just stood there."

"Can you think of where he might have been?"

"No."

"Nothing, son?"

"No. *Wait.*" He looked out the window, to the clear sky beyond.

"He pointed to a cloud. Yes, I remember. A beautiful cloud. Completely white. With a hole in it." Norm shook his head, as if he wanted to state that this story did not make a whole lot of sense to him either.

"A hole?"

"Yeah."

"A hole in the cloud?"

"Yep. Weird, isn't it?"

"I don't know. Maybe not."

"I don't know why though."

"Think. He didn't say a word to you?"

Norm scratched his head. "I don't think he said anything."

"Did you see anything in the hole?"

"Nope."

Norm hesitated and Brian noticed.

"Or beyond the hole, behind the cloud?"

"Something. I can't remember."

"Try to remember. Maybe it'll come back to you."

"No. Wait. I saw something written *on the cloud.*"

"Written?"

Norm had seen a name he could not remember, but he was sure it was a name of someone he did not recognize.

"Some name you didn't know?" his father pressed on.

"Yes. Just a name."

"Did it matter?"

"Somehow it was very important. I don't know why though."

"Then you have to try to remember."

"I know." He glanced to the window again. "Jeremy." He turned abruptly to his father. "The name was Jeremy. It's strange. I don't even know a Jeremy."

Brian sat speechless. He and his wife had decided years ago not to mention Norm's uncle who had died in infancy. Not only did Norm not know his uncle's name, he did not know of his existence in the first place. His parents did not want to scare him. Death occupied too much of a front row seat in their family already.

Brian finished telling me his story with a curious mixture of joy and bewilderment on his face.

"Did you tell Norm about your Jeremy?" I asked him.

"He could tell we knew a Jeremy. We told him….I think he'll be in good company up there, don't you?" he asked.

As if "no" could have been the answer to that question.

"I sure think he will. And when it's time for you to go, you'll see a hole in another one of those clouds."

"Any inscriptions for me?"

"Welcome home, son-slash-dad. All three united."

FOUR

RED DRAGONFLIES

The principle illness of man is his restless
Curiosity of those things he cannot know.

BLAISE PASCAL, PENSÉES

———————————————————

If at first, the idea is not absurd
Then there is no hope for it.

ALBERT EINSTEIN

Thirty-seven years passed before I fully grasped that Christ did not only pledge to send the Holy Spirit, but that he made good on his word. In a little bit I want to tell you my personal take on this miraculous story. That experience shattered my preconceived notions of this world. I finally comprehended that God, in his great mercy and grace, sent his son to redeem a fallen humanity, and that this fallen humanity included me!

As far as messengers or mail from heaven, I didn't know anyone else would or could communicate from the beyond. However, one of my little friends, whose name was Dwight, did promise an update after his death. His days on earth, he knew, were numbered. He later sent a postcard to back up that preposterous claim.

Let me describe to you how that came about. But I need help, and for that I will ask another remarkable young man named Stanley. He and Dwight were unlikely friends, for they possessed little in common beyond their age—give or take a few months—and a diagnosis of cancer. Dwight owned plenty of brains and a fertile imagination. In contrast, a devastating genetic disorder called Wolf-Hirschhorn disease kept Stanley wheelchair-bound, and he possessed no means, short of a smile or a sad expression, to let others know he understood what they told him. However, one day he raised his thumbs, quite to everyone's surprise, after I had asked him to do just that if he felt well that morning.

At twelve years of age, he had reportedly outlived all other children with his condition. Forget the fact that he also survived leukemia—not once, but twice. Then a fungal infection of his left forearm threatened to eat away the tendon he needed to move his thumb. This was a cruel joke by all accounts that nature played on him. Intervention by a hand surgeon and a year of antibiotics allowed him to keep a smidgen of function in his hand.

His mother brought him for a follow-up visit a few months after he had completed all therapy.

Thumbs up! Stanley signaled contentment. His mother immediately poured out her heart, reporting this first part of her story. Stanley came to her in a dream, not as the invalid in the wheelchair in front of us, but as an attractive fellow with red-blond hair in his early to mid-twenties. She recognized him before he uttered a single word. He told her he felt tired of being locked up in his decrepit body, and weary of his inability to express his love and thanks for the many years she had cared for him. He came to say he was fine, regardless of the fact that *on this earth* he remained frozen in the old helpless self.

His mother pointed out that this encounter with her son could not have been more real than her conversation was with me. I did not tell her that I wondered—and perhaps you do, too—whether this dream simply signified an expression of wishful thinking on her part. As if she could read my mind, she continued by asking whether I remembered Dwight.

How could I not? Dwight left his mark, on her and on me as much as on everyone else. Nobody could forget his gentle nature and the hopefulness he displayed in the many dark moments of his treatments, despite the odds stacked against him. His family did not own much, but it gave him and his parents great pleasure to share the lychees and other exotic fruit his father had been harvesting for years in the orchards around their home. For a while the germ cell tumor in his chest responded to aggressive therapy, but it came back a year later and cut short his life.

Stanley's mother reported an encounter she once had with Dwight when she sat at his bedside at a time that both boys were in the hospital.

"Are you scared," she asked him? They had openly talked about difficult issues in the past and felt no need to keep the topic of death out of their conversation.

"No," Dwight did not have reason to be scared. "I'll be fine in heaven!"

His certainty surprised her. "How can you be so sure?" she asked him.

He knew, he asserted. And he would let her know, once he got there.

She was baffled. "How are you going to do that?"

After a few seconds of reflection, he said he would send her red dragonflies.

She said she had never seen red dragonflies, never in her life, green and brown and blue ones, yes, but not red ones; she did not even know they existed in the first place.

Neither did I. Did you?

Two weeks after his death, she happened to walk into her back yard. Swarms of dragonflies, too numerous to count, danced and caroused above her, each and every one of them red, spreading their gorgeous color over the blue canvas of the sky.

As if to confirm the story, the local newspaper published a photo one of its readers had submitted not long thereafter. On a rich green leaf of a palm tree perched a red dragonfly, spreading its wings in absolute stillness.

———————

Dark gray curtains shielded the hospital bed from the door and the hallway beyond. A lamp mounted on the wall above the head of a single bed spilled cold light, illuminating the sparsely furnished room. A young girl lay restless, groaning in pain every so often. She held her mother's hand in a tight grip as her surgeon explained the procedure he planned to perform the next morning.

"I'm scared, mom," Brandi said.

"Oh Honey, don't be. Everything will be all right," her mother answered, hope and fear fighting for supremacy in her mind. Brandi's pelvis harbored a terrible threat. Her mother did not want to mention the word cancer and frighten Brandi any more than necessary. She felt as if someone was tearing her heart out of her chest.

Later, she did not show surprise when the surgery confirmed her worst suspicions. She had so many questions yet feared the answers. More than that, she had an inkling she might not find any answers at all.

When Brandi of all people reminded her of their faith in the Lord, a glimmer of promise brightened the stark, dreary room.

I met Brandi and her family a few weeks later. They came from a town more than two hours south of our hospital but never complained of the burden all this frequent and prolonged travel caused them. Brandi did not, at a superficial glance, appear different from any other girl her age. She was eleven years old and very pretty, and she acted and talked much like everyone else around her. Only the bald head under her printed scarf and the metal bump on her chest wall, an intravenous device her surgeon had implanted under the skin, made her stand out.

Brandi had embarked on a journey that would leave her life and that of her parents turned upside down. Dull and aching pains in her left hip had been bothering her for weeks. An unrelenting pressure to urinate caused even worse discomfort. Every half-hour she emptied small amounts but experienced short-lived relief at best. After urine tests ruled out a bladder infection, X-rays revealed destruction of her hipbones. A large mass extending into her pelvis compressed the bladder to a thin, flat pouch.

A biopsy of her tumor revealed the beautifully blue yet horribly destructive cells common to a number of childhood cancers. Further studies established the diagnosis of Ewing sarcoma, which is a bone tumor that primarily occurs in adolescents and young adults.

Brandi's world fell apart when a physician recommended the removal of her leg, hip and half her pelvis as her best option. She wanted to live if that option still existed, but not under those circumstances. Nobody would want to look at her with half her lower body missing. Nobody would see her with thoughts other than those of pity—and pity was the last thing in the world she wanted.

Her family sought an alternative that could spare her the mutilation and humiliation such surgery would cause, and leave her with the humanity of a body not cut into pieces.

Another option did exist, an option that makes long-term survival possible for many patients like Brandi. The combination of chemotherapy, limited surgery and radiation often proves curative in cases such as hers. Brandi and her parents felt they could agree to this therapy. It lent them hope, and it lent Brandi the certainty that she would still recognize herself in the mirror at the end of her treatments.

Over time, her pain resolved, and she could urinate again without problems. For the next year her life followed a constant up and down. She received chemotherapy every three weeks and in between required care for the many complications patients typically encounter as a consequence of such aggressive treatment. Fevers and infections alternated with episodes of nausea and vomiting. Ulcers in her mouth and throat made eating impossible. Radiation to her pelvis caused a bad skin burn and bouts of diarrhea, but a different, redeemed future was worth the fear and the pain. *It had to be,* if only she could hang on through all the pain and discouragement.

Further biopsies of her hip showed the tumor gone and promised an end to her suffering. Mercifully, only scar tissue remained of what once threatened her limb and her existence. Brandi and her parents were elated that life would now be normal again, and she reported exuberantly to me on her new experiences. Her hair grew back thick and beautiful. She returned to school, she worshiped her Lord and visited her friends, and she behaved like any other twelve or thirteen-year-old does.

One night around one o'clock, her mother called. Brandi complained of nausea, vomiting and diarrhea again. She had no fever or pain, and the description of her illness fit the bill of a simple stomach virus. After giving her mother a few instructions—clear liquids, then a mild diet and attention to her urine output to detect dehydration—I heard nothing but silence.

"Are you there?" I asked, upon which her mother began to describe once more in great detail Brandi's problems. I felt too tired to complain that I had already heard that same story and given thorough instructions, so I proceeded to outline my recommendations again. When I got to the hydration issues, I suddenly realized that I was speaking German. Brandi's mother, one of the sweetest and most polite people I know, did not want to interrupt, believing I needed to clarify to my wife what I was doing in the middle of the night. With egg on my face, I explained for a third time. In English.

Ten months after the end of therapy, Brandi returned to us again with fever, hip pain and swollen lymph nodes in her groin. The tumor had recurred, or so it appeared at first glance.

Instead of the small, round cells, a biopsy of one of the nodes revealed big, lumpy, ugly cells. Another biopsy, this time of her pelvic bone, confirmed Brandi suffered from a different malignancy, an unusual lymph cancer in the location of her prior bone tumor.

"How is this possible?" Brandi's mother asked with tears in her eyes.

"I don't know," I answered quietly, not sure what else to say.

"Have you ever seen anything like this?"

Neither my colleagues nor I had ever encountered a situation such as

Brandi's surprising case. Nor could we find reports in the medical literature.

"Are you sure?" she asked.

"Well…"

It must have been easy to notice my hesitation. In candor, nobody felt sure. One of my colleagues contacted a leading expert on childhood lymphoma in the country and described the findings. "You must have screwed up," the expert nonchalantly responded. She is not known to mince words. Perhaps she had hit the nail on the head. Perhaps someone had made a mistake. A bad mistake.

Treatment of a first cancer occasionally causes a second malignancy, months or years later. Radiation therapy can induce other bone tumors. Chemotherapy sometimes leads to leukemia. But Brandi's type of lymphoma had never arisen as a result of prior therapy for a bone tumor. In a reverse-case scenario, a teenager in Austria suffering from Brandi's type of lymphoma later developed Ewing sarcoma—although elsewhere in her body, but this information did not provide practical help either.

The most likely explanation was as simple as it was gut-wrenching: someone had made a terrible mistake. The two tumors were unambiguously different. Whatever features one tumor expressed, the other did not, and vice versa.

"Is it possible they could have been mixed up? What if the first specimen came from someone else and not from Brandi?" her father questioned with reasonable concern. The recent lymph node and bone biopsies showed identical results, which brought the original diagnosis into question.

Our colleagues in the pathology department went through their records. Another patient, a girl a few years younger than Brandi, had been diagnosed with the same bone tumor two days before Brandi. Their rooms had been right next to one another.

Those investigations provoked a scary thought: Brandi had always had a lymphoma and now a recurrence. We had misdiagnosed and inappropriately treated her for a cancer, which in actuality grew in another patient.

Regardless of the implications, the truth needed to emerge. The definitive answer came from a genetic analysis of the two tumor tissues as well as Brandi's blood cells. It proved unequivocal, irrefutable and surprising. Both tumors, with *absolute* certainty, came from Brandi's body.

The concern for her condition overshadowed the relief not to have "screwed up." Brandi would not tolerate the immensely aggressive, year-long treatment required to cure the lymphoma right after the therapy she had already endured in the recent past.

"We should consider a bone marrow transplant after two or three cycles of standard chemotherapy, assuming her tumor responds," I recommended. Review of Brandi's case left few other options. "We could see whether her sister is a donor. We might as well test the whole family."

"What's the chance that they'll match?" her father asked.

"Twenty-five percent." That did not represent an encouraging number by any stretch of the imagination, although it was better than no chance at all.

"That's all, is it?" the father continued, disappointed.

"What about us?" her mother wanted to know.

"One or two percent at best, unfortunately."

"What about the Ewing? Would a transplant prevent *that* from coming back?" her father asked.

"Well, I sure hope we've cured the Ewing by now, but yes, a transplant might be helpful if any such tumor cells remain anywhere in her body."

"I have nothing to lose then, do I?" Brandi chirped with sarcasm.

"If there's any chance at all, we should go for the transplant," her mother added with a determined, stoic face, ignoring her daughter's comment.

The analysis took a week. Her sister did not even come close, but her mother unexpectedly *did.* Though not a perfect donor, she felt convinced she would bestow on Brandi the gift of life for a second time.

A few days before the transplant, Brandi recorded a video of herself for her friends and her family. She wanted to express her faith and her hope in the Lord and share them with the people most important in her life. She was determined to fight but also committed to accept whatever outcome her Lord intended for her. Deep down, she knew the video might serve as a way to say good-bye if she did not survive.

Following a harrowing week of chemotherapy and radiation to her whole body, she received her mother's bone marrow. Mouth sores and ulcers developed. Brandi drooled incessantly because swallowing her saliva, let alone food, caused tremendous pain. Fevers ensued and then a blood infection. Episodes of nausea and vomiting gave way to diarrhea.

Within three weeks, her new bone marrow grew and made new blood cells. All her symptoms resolved entirely such that Brandi felt good enough to go home a month after the transplant. For all her family and her caregivers knew, the lymph cancer had vanished.

What advice could we give her other than to cherish her life and live it to the fullest? She planned to attend school again, and she looked forward to spending time among her many friends, her family and the people dear to her in her church. Many others besides her prayed the lymphoma would not come back after the nightmare she had gone through.

A year and a half later Brandi's mother stood in our clinic again, her face ashen gray. She knew this had to be the end. She knew the answer but still asked the question:

"There's nothing else we can do for her? No other chemo?" She shook her head as if to answer the question herself.

Brandi faced another relapse. Shingles sixteen months after the transplant suggested a weakening of her immune system, and she had not mentioned to her parents the discomfort she had been experiencing in her hip. The CAT scan results were merciless. A tumor was back. The unavoidable question that came along was: which one?

Could a third type of cancer be a possibility? Indeed, that question crossed many people's minds. Surprisingly, the Ewing sarcoma, which had lain dormant for over three years, had recurred, and not the lymphoma. Brandi could not possibly withstand more aggressive therapy of any type that might have a smitten of a chance to cure her cancer at this late state.

"Is there nothing we can do?" Brandi's mother asked.

"Nothing we haven't tried already," I answered, hesitating whether I should mention what reverberated through my mind. "We may be able to give her more chemotherapy and radiation, but I don't think she'll be able to handle much of either after all she's gone through already. At least it might buy her some time."

Several weeks earlier, the Tampa Tribune, a local newspaper, had approached our group with the request to write an editorial on the progress of therapy for childhood cancer. At the time, the papers nationwide contained a plethora of stories regarding a "new" concept of tumor therapy—therapy designed to interfere with the growth of blood vessels feeding the tumor and thus to starve it into submission. The strategy could not claim novelty. One man more than all others combined had laid the necessary groundwork for its application in humans.

For decades, Judah Folkman, a cancer investigator in Boston, had been studying and advocating ideas so simple that the medical establishment did not take them seriously until recently, convinced they could not and would not work. When enthusiasm suddenly spilled over, Dr. Folkman felt compelled to instill a sense of badly needed reality.

"I can cure your cancer," he said in an interview before he added laconically, "If you are a mouse." His prior experience was limited to tumor therapy of rodents that researchers had first injected with human cancer cells.

Nobody in our hospital knew anything about this type of therapy that promised to be so much more gentle than the standard cancer treatments that were then available. The newspaper's request triggered more investigation on our part. Nothing was known anywhere of human patients undergoing this kind of intervention. No one had ever reported anything of that nature.

An article published by a research group in Chicago attracted our attention. Investigators in that laboratory were able to create one of the potentially effective chemicals Dr. Folkman and his group had discovered in the mice. The procedure required nothing more than a single protein all humans carry in their blood stream, and two medications doctors commonly use in the treatment of high blood pressure and blood clots, respectively. If this worked in the culture dish in the laboratory, it could conceivably also work in the body of a human.

Could it work in Brandi?

I thought back to that gut-wrenching moment when Brandi's mother asked whether anything else existed that could be done to save her daughter's life. Did we have nothing left, anything that we had not tried yet?

On the day of her next follow-up appointment, I explained to them the thoughts and ideas percolating through my mind for a few days, although I did that with hesitation. Talking about mice and culture dishes to a patient who is dying of cancer seemed almost absurd. The treatment, if it deserved that name in the first place, might not work. It might make matters worse rather than better. Not only that, but the hospital required approval of the treatment before we could even proceed. A research committee would assess this investigational "mouse therapy" for its safety in human subjects.

"Has this ever been done before?" This question arose as the first of many during a rather stormy committee meeting.

"No. We only have the animal and culture data." No precedent for this existed.

"No documentation in the literature?" someone else asked.

A broad search had identified nothing, other than the limited information we had already provided, data more about mice than about men. A long discussion ensued. Issues of death and dying, human suffering, disease and health merged with questions about legal issues, biochemistry and conventional drug therapy. Despite a healthy skepticism among the committee members, none of the admittedly warranted concerns appeared insurmountable.

The objection that almost derailed the project before it got off the ground came from an unexpected direction.

"I don't think it's right to give people hope when there's no hope," one of the hospital's chaplains interjected. He, of all people, was the last person I would have expected to object to dispensing hope.

Who can live without hope? Nobody should die without at least a glimmer of hope—in the here and now, on this side of death or in life after death.

Brandi knew where to find this hope. She knew the evening before her first operation, before the diagnosis of her first cancer, when she encouraged her distraught mother. The Lord would accompany her, wherever she went. Back then he did, and now he would do it again. He would hold her in the palms of his hands.

The "treatment" received approval, the committee's objections and concerns notwithstanding. Two patients could receive the "voodoo medicine", as one of my colleagues labeled the approach, before the committee wanted an update on the therapy's progress. This we considered a fair deal, a deal we could abide by.

Brandi started her treatment, and nothing happened—until six weeks later when she developed high fevers and a newly swollen lymph node in the groin—in her left groin of all places. Blood and urine cultures revealed a bacterial infection. A CAT scan showed a pus pocket in the location of the prior tumor.

"I don't know, man," the radiologist commented, an astounded look in the corner of his eye. For years he had examined Brandi's CAT scans. "Where's the tumor?" he asked. I stood speechless.

A surgeon drained the pus from her pelvis and the tumor "disappeared." Brandi received antibiotics for a fortnight and recovered but continued her experimental treatments for a few months more.

"Can I go jogging now?" This question came as the most simple and straightforward, yet amazing one I had heard in a long time, from a girl who so recently had stared death squarely in the eye. She probably could as long as she jogged gently, although her brittle bones might not tolerate such strenuous, repetitive impact.

"Take it easy, will you?" we admonished her, as if she had any inclination to listen to that futile advice.

Brandi saw a specialist for hormone replacement therapy. The telephone call from the endocrinologist a few days later hardly could have been less worrisome. "It's probably nothing, but looking at your patients, I never know. I sent her for an ultrasound," she said dryly. She could feel a tiny nodule in Brandi's thyroid gland. I wanted to brush off my concerns as unwarranted suspicions, but intuitively I felt them justified.

"Probably nothing", in light of her odyssey, more than likely meant "probably something". The nodule appeared to be a simple cyst, but nobody accepted that interpretation without further studies. None of several subsequent tests helped to answer our nagging questions. But inaction seemed to carry more risk than surgery, and so our brave young lady went back to the operating room. By now, she knew this place as intimately as she did her own living room.

Brandi's family showed no astonishment when they learned of Brandi's thyroid cancer. The radiation before her transplant may have caused this third tumor. We asked experts in genetic medicine for their advice but they could not come up with any useful insight either.

Brandi's resilience through all of this proved astounding. Every time something tipped her over, she got back up on her feet right away. Her surgeon removed the thyroid gland before Brandi underwent treatment with radioactive iodine. She took it without a hint of complaint.

Following estrogen therapy, she felt better than she ever did in the four years prior. Dating moved to the forefront of her mind as well as a driver's license, visits to the mall and the movies. Life still tasted sweet. It usually does at the age of sixteen.

More than another year after her surprising recovery, the pain in her left hip returned. For the third time around, the bone tumor was back. Brandi felt tired, tired of fighting, tired of living, and tired of seeing death lose one round after the other, only to sneak back into her life as soon as she let down her guard.

One day, Brandi declared rather abruptly, "Mom, I'll never get to plan my wedding. I want to plan my funeral." Her parents found this matter difficult to think let alone speak openly about, but they honored her request.

The resumption of the investigational therapy would have been an option but Brandi no longer expressed an interest in that. She wanted to spend her energy on her funeral while she still enjoyed that option. She knew her death lurked very close by. Only with great difficulty could she get up and move around. Soon her disease would sap her of her last physical strength.

"Mom, I'm scared," Brandi told her mother.

"Oh Honey, don't be. You'll be all right up there in heaven." Her mother pointed to the ceiling of their living room.

"*Mom!* I'm not talking about *that!* I'm afraid nobody'll come to my *funeral*." Her mother did not know whether to laugh or to cry.

Three weeks later, Brandi went home to her Lord. Her fears were unwarranted, as more than a thousand people attended her funeral. The procession to her grave stretched two and a half miles long. Many received a goodbye letter from her.

I thank God for the extra years he gave me, she wrote. I am now in heaven and dancing.

Then Brandi spoke at her funeral.

She had asked her parents to show the video she had made before the transplant. For her, death meant heaven, and heaven was not a place to fear but to cherish.

There is no doubt in anyone's mind that she's there now, dancing and enjoying her two healthy legs.

FIVE

DEATH OF A DISEASE

The mind has a thousand eyes,
And the heart but one;
Yet the light of a whole life dies
When love is done.

FRANCIS WILLIAM BOURDILLON, THE NIGHT HAS A THOUSAND EYES

As more exposed to suffering and distress;
Thence also, more alive to tenderness.

WILLIAM WORDSWORTH, THE HAPPY WARRIOR

Death is part of every life as the night is part of the day—neither exists without the other. It is an inevitable element of every man's journey, whether he cares to embrace it or wishes to ignore it. It is firmly implanted in the first seed of a life long before this life is even aware of its own existence. To think it might be different is foolishness. Man's hope does not rest in the avoidance of death but in the prospect of overcoming it. Death is not the end of a futile path; rather, it is a mere step on a far greater journey.

Modern medicine fosters the illusion that things might be otherwise. Ultimately, it does nothing but postpone—often at great human costs—what it cannot change. The loss of a child is a difficult component of the work of a children's cancer doctor. The death of a disease, on the other hand, is a far more unusual event.

Scotty, a small four-year-old with a pixie-like face, lay quietly in his bed. He was alone in a two-patient room in the children's hospital where I had been working for the last two years.

"Hi Scotty," I said, introducing myself as I entered, uncertain what to expect. Scotty did not respond.

"How are you doing?"

Scotty produced an unintelligible grunt.

Bouts of vomiting caused profound dehydration. His skin showed a tinge of gray and his eyes were sunken in his orbits. A salt water solution dripped into the vein of his forearm.

"They asked me to take a look at you and figure out what's wrong."

Again, he said nothing.

"Are you hurting? Is that why you're not talking to me?"

Just a hint of a nod seemed to affirm my suspicion.

"I'm sorry. I hope we'll make you all better very soon."

Scotty's breathing sounds came fast and shallow, while his heart raced like that of a runner on an uphill course. Loud whooshing, gurgling sounds emerged from his obstructed intestines. My examination of his belly made Scotty respond abruptly.

"Don't do that. That hurts!"

The vehemence and clarity of his comeback after utter silence struck me as comical, the seriousness of his illness notwithstanding. Scotty turned out to be the sweetest and most engaging child I had met in a long time. Only when he fell ill did he come across as a man of few but harsh words.

He had been admitted to the hospital because he suffered from nausea, vomiting and abdominal pain. The X-rays showed that his intestines were obstructed. That problem likely resulted from scar tissue that had developed after a prior operation. Unfortunately, Scotty was no stranger to surgery. He had barely left his mother's womb when he found his way to the operating room for the first time.

Back then his skull appeared very elongated and deformed, and the water-containing channels in his brain did not flow freely. Without correction, the pressure in his brain would have increased to a dangerous level and it likely would have killed him. A neurosurgeon inserted a plastic shunt to bypass the obstruction.

A malformation at the end of his gut turned out to be equally problematic. Scotty was born without an anus. Another surgeon created an artificial opening, enabling Scotty to have normal bowel movements. In addition, he missed his left thumb, and only a useless stub of a digit protruded from his right hand.

This constellation of malformations led to the diagnosis of a rare genetic syndrome known as VACTERL. The mnemonic stands for abnormalities of the vertebrae, anus, heart, trachea and esophagus, kidneys and limbs. His first-born brother died shortly after birth due to multiple defects and deformities.

When Scotty's younger sister came along with similar problems, the doctor was convinced the children suffered from a different disorder than the originally suspected condition. Two physicians in the 1950's described the abnormalities Scotty and his siblings displayed. The new diagnosis, Baller-Gerold syndrome, carried the names of these two physicians. In essence, it summarized the abnormalities without saying a single thing about their cause.

That first day I saw Scotty, I knew very little about either of these extremely rare syndromes. The official reason for my consultation was a low platelet count in his blood stream. Platelets prevent bruising and bleeding, and surgery would have been dangerous without an adequate number of them. A review of the literature revealed that no patient with either syndrome ever developed low platelets. However, a third condition, namely Fanconi anemia, which is a rare bone marrow disorder, could explain the combination of all these abnormalities. Under the microscope, Scotty's marrow glared back half-empty. These findings fit exactly with what one would expect to see in a patient with this disease. Additional blood tests showed the brittle chromosomes characteristic of the disorder. His sister's marrow looked exactly the same.

Scotty received a platelet transfusion, and uneventful surgery restored normal bowel function. After he recovered, he transformed into the sweetest boy around and charmed everyone he encountered with intelligence and kindness.

Things changed drastically when he developed an infection and required hospitalization once more.

"Leave me alone!" He sounded adamant.

"Scotty, you know I have to examine you."

"No you don't."

"Yes I do."

"But I don't want you to."

"Don't you want me to make you better?"

"I don't care."

"I think you do."

"No I don't."

"I know a tough question for a smart boy like you. I bet you can't answer it. Shawn couldn't either."

Shawn was receiving treatment in a room down the hallway. He and Scotty had met in the clinic and in the hospital on a number of occasions. Scotty turned around. My comment made him too curious to resist the temptation to upstage his friend, and I possessed his full attention.

"If I ask you, you need to let me check out your heart and lungs."

"And my belly, too?"

"Yes, your belly, too, but I'm going to be very gentle, OK?"

He mouthed a hesitant OK.

"Here it is. Is what I'm going to tell you true or correct?"

"True."

"Wait a minute. I haven't told you yet."

"Oh."

"I'm going to tell you now. While you think for a moment, I'll check you out."

"OK."

"At night, it's colder than outside."

Lines on Scotty's forehead showed that he was thinking furiously. The nonsensical statement, which has put a frown on many foreheads, gave me the time I needed to complete the examination.

"All right, what's your answer? True or correct?"

"True."

"Smart move. How did you know that?"

"I knew."

He crossed his arms over his chest and with an air of pride he turned away, rolling his eyes and beaming victory.

Our study of the medical literature revealed that another patient with Baller-Gerold syndrome later received the corrected diagnosis of Fanconi anemia. We speculated that the first might simply be a severe form of the latter at a stage before such patients develop blood defects. In the end, we wrote a report of Scotty and his sister and sent it to a journal specializing in genetic medicine. The editor accepted it and forwarded it to two experts in the field with the following comment. "Dear Mike/Helga—the Baller-Gerold syndrome is dying fast—any funeral orations you want to offer?"

Funeral orations did follow, and soon they buried a disease. Death of a disease is less emotional than that of a patient. No one shed tears. In the meantime, Scotty continued his treatments.

Months later, he returned once again to the hospital. This time he coughed and fevered with pneumonia. Antibiotics, oxygen and tender, loving care got him back on his feet. The next time I saw him, however, his mood had not quite caught up with his healing lungs, and Scotty ignored me steadfastly.

"Scotty, good morning."

"Nnh," he grunted.

"How are you doing today?"

"Nnh."

"You're not talking to me?"

"Nnh."

"Scotty, you have to help me out here."

Scotty turned brusquely, and staring me down, commanded, "Get out of *your* face right now!"

I burst out laughing. "How am I going to do that?"

My disrespect for his feelings angered Scotty even more.

"I don't care. Just get out of *your* face right now," he repeated, crossed his arms over his chest and turned away in disgust. I knew enough to leave Scotty alone for the moment. In the afternoon, his mood improved enough that our fractured relationship could mend again.

SIX

GOD IS GREAT

We want a few mad people now.
See where the sane ones have landed us.

George Bernard Shaw, St. Joan

Most medical conditions today have standard and effective therapies. Some disorders, however, are so rare that no generally accepted treatments exist. Others are more common but unresponsive to the medications we have at our disposal. Many cancers still fall into this latter category, and medical progress is often unacceptably slow. Under such circumstances, one may have to look outside the box and venture beyond conventional wisdom. Marcel Proust, the French novelist, identified such a paradigm shift when he said the real voyage of discovery consists not in seeking new landscapes but in having new eyes. Here are the stories of three young children in desperate need of a fresh perspective. "New eyes" led to astounding results. In one instance it even took an ineffective treatment to save a life. Divine hands may very well have played a role.

I need to go back more than forty years to introduce you to those new eyes. At the time, I was in seventh grade and growing up in Germany. A local newspaper reported on a boy suffering from recurrent leukemia, who could no longer receive treatment in the hospital of our hometown. Bone marrow transplantation provided his best option. For this treatment, which sounded so extraordinary at the time, he needed to go to Seattle. Seattle, leukemia and marrow transplantation were all non-entities for me at that time, but the complexity of this scenario intrigued me enough to want to learn about such diseases and treatments. Nineteen years later, after medical school and residency in pediatrics, I got that privilege during subspecialty training at the University of Washington.

The outwardly preposterous insight of a great man turned out to be a great blessing. That knowledge came in quite handy in the care of the children mentioned above.

I admire people who are willing to fight for their convictions despite great risks to their careers, their health, or their lives, and bring their goals to fruition.

In the political world Vaclav Havel, Aung San Suu Kyi and more recently the Nobel Peace Prize winners Kailash Satyarthi and Malala Yousafzai come to mind. In the medical field, Don Thomas stands at the top of my list. With his decades-long efforts, which were harshly criticized and ridiculed for years, he proved that marrow transplantation is feasible and effective. Any doubt was put to rest when Stockholm awarded him the Nobel Prize in medicine in 1990. Even more so, the myriad of children and adults who are now cured of close to a hundred diseases are a tribute to his life's work.

Some individuals are able to summarize a complicated aspect of life in simple yet elegant terms. Dr. Thomas gave an example that has stuck with me for twenty-five years. He faced a simple question at the end of a presentation to a large audience. One of his admirers asked about the suitability of marrow transplantation for an obscure disease of the nervous system. Dr. Thomas reflected for two seconds.

"George," he said, with a good portion of dry humor shining through, "You know my opinion. Bone marrow transplantation is good for everything."

Such conviction might at first consideration appear more ludicrous and absurd than one would expect from a serious scientist and physician. Yet, a growing number of reports suggest that marrow stem cells can create new heart, liver or brain tissue and cure many more diseases than those currently considered indications for transplantation.

Hippocrates, the father of modern medicine, once said, "Healing is a matter of time, but it is sometimes also a matter of opportunity." One of my patients came close to running out of time on more than one occasion. According to Hippocrates, we needed to look harder for an opportunity on the little boy's behalf. Don Thomas defined such an opportunity.

Ashraf's mother resigned herself to the inevitable: her son would not survive. She had kept a diary ever since the first day of his young and precious, yet so miserable life. With a heavy heart, she wrote a new entry in the diary: *"Met with Dr. Maloney and staff. Ashraf's bone marrow is completely fibrosis. No cells was found. So don't treat his ear infection and let it cause his death."*

A sad smile spread over her face as she realized, astounded, how much her English had improved. In her own written words, she summed up the essence of her son's desperate situation. At least she could now understand the doctor, although it pained her to listen to him. Dr. Maloney came across as a caring, thoughtful man. When she questioned him whether Ashraf would die, he looked at her and her husband as if weighing whether they were ready for his response or destined to suffocate in their despair. Nodding his head, he answered with a deep, grave voice,

"Yes, he's going to die. If not this time, then likely the next."

She and her husband were ready for the answer. They knew the truth. The one question Dr. Maloney could not answer was why. They asked him many times. More often than that, they asked themselves, never to find what they were looking for. Only God, she rested assured, knew the answer.

Ashraf could not go on living half the time and dying the other. He had already lost the inside of one ear and the bone behind it. Now he would lose his other ear, and more likely his life. None of the many medications his doctors had prescribed over the last year improved, let alone cured, his underlying illness. None proved suitable to prevent one horrific infection after the other. His parents wondered whether it would be better to let Ashraf die in peace and prevent him from suffering any longer, as some friends suggested.

The family wrestled with their decision for days before they decided to continue therapy to give Ashraf one last chance. He rested in God's hands; either God would let him live, or he would call Ashraf home to himself.

To his parents' amazement as much as to his physicians', Ashraf hung on by a bare thread for a while before he improved enough to leave the intensive care unit. He lost his left eardrum, although the surrounding bones remained intact. But it would only be a matter of time before the next infection completed the destruction this one had threatened to accomplish.

Ashraf's mother had born her son four months prematurely. His parents had always looked at his survival as nothing but a miracle. A breathing machine supported him for weeks because his lungs were poorly developed. Eye damage proved a minor issue, and intestinal problems extremely premature babies often experience resolved with little intervention.

The absence of white blood cells, in contrast, did not fit the bill. And this problem did not improve. He sat defenseless against overwhelming infections akin to a duck with clipped wings in hunting season. Fibrous scar tissue crowded out the marrow where the blood-forming elements should have been. Then too, the peculiar form of his red cells could not have been more befitting. Instead of the normal doughnut-like appearance, his were tear-shaped, eager to make their silent contribution to bemoan Ashraf's doomed existence.

Moving out of state, the family sought medical care elsewhere. The parents proceeded nervously because Dr. Maloney had always taken care of Ashraf. However, leaving contained one positive aspect: another doctor might come up with a different diagnosis or, more importantly, with a different idea of how to treat the disease. Those hopes soon evaporated. Although the family found caring and compassionate help, the answers remained elusive. The repeated use of the medications that previously proved futile made no difference. Again the why found no answer.

Ashraf continued to live—if the way he spent his days could be construed as living. His parents kept him locked up at home for fear he might contract an infection during even a casual encounter with others. Yet he did develop infections despite his forced seclusion and spent weeks at a time in the hospital. Moreover, he now required red blood cell and platelet transfusions with increasing frequency.

His two cute brothers, in turn, ran around healthy, and their blood counts never dropped below normal levels. An occasional cold in the winter constituted the worst that ever happened to them.

The family moved to Florida when Ashraf turned three years old. His parents refused to give up hope, and Ashraf refused to die. The more transfusions he received, the less his blood counts increased. This therapy became the proverbial Sisyphus work, an effort in futility like a bucket being filled with water that drains through a hole at the bottom. His swollen spleen trapped the transfused red cells and platelets and held on to them for dear life instead of allowing them to circulate in the bloodstream where they could fulfill their purpose.

A surgeon removed Ashraf's spleen and biopsied the enlarged liver and a lymph node. The examination of these tissues led to striking discoveries. The bones remained empty of marrow cells, but the organs were full of them. Ashraf's body made blood cells in all these organs, although far less efficiently than inside his bones which God designed for this purpose.

The unusual constellation of findings suggested a surprising diagnosis, which is seen almost exclusively in adults beyond sixty years of age. The disorder carried the unusual name of Agnogenic Myeloid Metaplasia, or AMM. To our knowledge, it had been reported only five times in children. A Turkish boy carried the diagnosis, as did an American and three Saudi Arabian children, two of them siblings. Their doctors suspected a genetically determined, congenital disease, not an acquired one as that in adults.

Two years before Ashraf came, I read about the three Saudi children. Surprised by the oddity of the diagnosis and the rarity of the condition, I pondered throwing away the report. The illogical thought that we would encounter the disease if we got rid of its description led me to keep the publication.

Ashraf finally had a diagnosis, obscure as that might be. Topping off the surreal experience, Ashraf's family came from the United Arab Emirates, although no biologic relationship to the three young Saudis described in the article existed. We could not elicit a family history of the disorder, or any disease. The parents were reluctant to talk, as if having this disorder meant a stigma, an embarrassment.

Precious little time remained in Ashraf's case. If marrow transplantation proved good enough for everything, it ought to be good enough for Ashraf. Both brothers matched him perfectly, and both maintained normal marrow function and blood counts. The older of the two became his donor. Fourteen days after transplantation, Ashraf's blood circulated more white blood cells than ever before in his life. The scar tissue in his marrow spaces melted away like an ice cube in the sun, and he went home a healthy young man. An ear surgeon reconstructed his left eardrum, and a hearing aid allows Ashraf to communicate. These days, the rare common cold is all that ever really bothers him.

His schoolteacher phoned more than ten years later. I almost laughed out loud when I heard what she wanted to tell me. "Ashraf is too hyperactive. You need to give him a prescription for Ritalin or something like that. He can't sit still." She may be correct. Ashraf may need help. But these days, we are simply grateful that Ashraf is alive.

For a very short while, people thought that Ashraf's discharge from the transplant unit provided the end to a great story. But behold, the story came with a sequel.

On the day of Ashraf's departure from the hospital, his father took me aside.

"You'll get a call from my brother in Denver. We told him yesterday about Ashraf's transplant," he said.

"You haven't told him until now?"

"No, nothing. He had no idea."

"Why not?"

"We thought we'd better wait and see how things turned out."

"I hope he'll be pleased. When did he last see Ashraf?"

"Not for quite a while."

"What's he going to talk to me about?"

"He has a daughter. Mona. She's six years old. She's got the same disease."

"You are serious?"

He nodded.

"Why didn't you ever tell me?"

"We don't talk much in my family."

Half his family did not know Ashraf or his cousin were seriously ill.

"She has the same disease, and you never told me?"

He ignored the question and countered with a simple statement. "She has a brother and a sister."

"And you think we should type them and transplant her?"

"Sure. Why not? It worked for my son. Why wouldn't it work for her?" He posed a good question. Why not? What did we have to lose?

This rare condition in Ashraf and Mona supported the concept of AMM as a genetic disorder–if not in children in general, than at least in Arabic children. Interestingly enough, their fathers were brothers, and their mothers were sisters.

Mona's two siblings proved to be perfect matches, and the older became her donor. Nine years after her transplant, Mona is a beautiful and healthy girl. Once a year or so, the family calls to find out whether she can get this immunization or that vaccine. She has not developed much more than an occasional cold either. God is the Lord of mighty grace.

———————————

Perhaps the most difficult situation a pediatric cancer doctor faces is the moment when he has to tell parents that no therapy exists to cure their child. Nobody wants to give up or let go. At what point is it reasonable to shift gears from curative treatments to end-of-life care?

In the early 1960's, the survival rate for the common form of childhood leukemia, which happens to also be the most frequent cancer, amounted to a giant four percent. Ninety-six out of a hundred children died either due to treatment-related complications or, most commonly, succumbed to recurrent disease. Attempts to treat these children did not make a whole lot of sense back then. Yet some people in our field showed tremendous stubbornness. Fortunately, they pursued new alternatives despite the odds. Today almost ninety percent of these children survive. This is one of the most phenomenal success stories of modern medicine, if not of all medicine, and yet it is almost unknown to most people.

It was not all that long after my experience with Ashraf and Mona that I ran into one of those difficult situations. Beverly was a seven-year-old tomboy full of life and spunkiness. You would love her smile and her quick wit.

Beverly presented with melanoma. This most serious form of skin cancer is almost unheard-of in children. Not only did she have a large tumor on her scalp that a surgeon in another hospital resected, although without the appropriate wide, safe margins. Her disease had already spread to the lymph glands in her neck, and a CAT scan documented multiple lesions in her lungs as well. By any criteria, her prognosis was dismal. Not knowing how to proceed in the most reasonable way, I looked for advice from some of my colleagues with different expertise. Dr. Berger, one of our plastic surgeons, happened to be around. I asked him whether at some later point more extensive scalp surgery might be indicated if we were able to shrink her disease in the other locations. Our conversation could not have been more brief or disappointing.

"There's no sense in doing this kind of surgery. She'll die no matter what we do," he said. He is a very good surgeon. I respect him and admire the way he works but he made me upset because I could not accept that we had to throw in the towel.

"She'll die anyway." Why waste time and money, he said, why take risks for a universally dismal outcome? He could provide his services and do the best job in the world, and all the efforts would still be fruitless.

"They all die. It makes no sense. Zippo," said another plastic surgeon who did not know about the statements of his colleague. "Nobody survives."

"You don't want to try? There are a few people in the literature who survived."

After five cycles of chemotherapy, CAT scans no longer showed the tumors in her lungs, and the mass in her neck shrunk. An ear surgeon removed sixty-eight separate lymph glands from Beverly's neck. Tests revealed that thirty-two of them still contained the cancer. The chemotherapy had obviously not destroyed all viable disease. Most certainly, tumor cells remained after the surgery. They had to be somewhere in her scalp, neck or lungs.

The internet proved to be a valuable asset at that moment. It allowed us to scan hundreds of up-to-date scientific papers relevant to the treatment of melanoma. An adult cancer specialist at the NIH, the National Institutes of Health, hinted at a possible beneficial effect of bone marrow transplantation in this devastating disease, although his experience was rather limited. You recall Dr. Thomas' timeless comment. If bone marrow transplantation is good for everything…

Unusual situations demand unusual solutions. Beverly had three siblings, one of whom turned out to be a perfect match, and the transplant triggered no complications. Years later, Beverly remains free of disease.

Six months after her procedure, the physician from the NIH presented an extensive update on his findings at an international conference. Quite a few patients with kidney cancer but none of the adult melanoma patients benefited.

For Beverly's sake, we learned "too late" of these results. Had we known them sooner, Beverly would not have undergone her transplant, and I do not think she would be here today. In addition, our surgical colleagues would have been correct in saying, "they all die." They rejoice with us that Beverly proved them wrong.

SEVEN

RARE THINGS ARE RARE

This is, I believe, the fundamental rule of life:
Life is not like this. It is very different.

KURT TUCHOLSKY

A sage who held that the earth is round,
And that it moves round the sun. What
An utter fool. Couldn't he use his eyes?

GEORGE BERNARD SHAW, ST. JOAN

I'm sure of nothing but the uncertain,
Baffled by nothing but the evident.
I'm doubtful of nothing but the sure,
I regard knowledge as mere accident.

FRANCOIS VILLON, POEMS

Physicians in the United States need to participate in Continuing Medical Education in order to keep their licenses to practice medicine. This requirement allows doctors to maintain their skills and knowledge in their ever-advancing fields of work. I have greatly benefited from a number of conferences and seminars and would not want to miss them. Some of the best pearls of wisdom with practical application, however, came from an entirely different source: children's books. Just a warning up front: if the following story sounds a bit crazy, well yes, it is, but bear with me!

One statement that has come up at least two dozen times in my medical career is this: "If it looks and walks and quacks like a duck, it's a duck." Medical wisdom. Undisputed.

But wait a minute! I've fallen flat on my face a bunch of times with that wisdom. But I've never gone wrong with what the Berenstein children's books taught me. Here's one example: "The things, they are deceiving."

Shopping at the local grocery store is a wonderful thing. Don't you love to chat with the little old ladies in the aisles who so diligently advertise tasty tidbits of food or drink nobody ever buys? I marvel at the endless lines of cereals, meats and produce, and I can easily imagine why people new to this bountiful country feel overwhelmed at first. Choice is only easy when one is used to having options. I glance at the section of the international foods and the colorful flags of the different countries supplying the delicacies displayed, and my mind wanders off to faraway places.

The greatest delight in the grocery store comes at the checkout counter where one can obtain the most valuable information. The paper scrolls with horoscopes deserve mention. For fifty cents anyone can learn about his or her future. Fifty cents is a bargain for the wealth of information ready at one's fingertips. How much would one not pay to avoid the costliest mistakes of one's life, or jump on the most rewarding investment opportunities if one identified the time as ripe and the celestial constellations favorably aligned?

Next to the horoscopes, magazines with the day-to-day updates of the lives of the soap opera stars catch my eye. These are more expensive but also more relevant. Especially in medicine, continuing education is everything.

Last but not least, the black and white papers most people perceive as too outrageous to take seriously demand my attention. I have to confess I did consider them ridiculous, a long time ago. But I changed my mind, and you ought to reconsider, too.

Granted, whether it is essential to know where Elvis got his hair cut last week may be debatable. Few of these stories are worthwhile reading material. But some are! Look at the mysterious stories about women, for example. Not too long ago, I read about a ninety-year-old lady giving birth to triplets. Not possible, you say?

Why not? A scientist, I suppose, would consider her an anomaly or an outlier. But so what? Does the exception prove its impossibility? Sarah, of Genesis' fame, had already lived ninety years when she conceived Isaac, and the world has never been the same.

I'm a pediatrician, not a geriatrician, and admittedly I don't know much about older ladies. The other day, while putting food on the conveyor belt, I read about a pregnant woman who delivered a cabbage.

A cabbage! Preposterous? I might have agreed, until recently. Listen to this before you make up your mind…

At fifteen years of age, Ashley brimmed with beauty in her physical appearance and in her demeanor and maturity. She did not always look this good. In fact, she was almost dead once. But I would rather remember her story from the end than from the beginning. Frankly, I had forgotten about the beginning.

Ashley returned for a routine check-up five months after completion of her therapy for lymphoma. Things were going well. She got good grades in school, and she got along with her obnoxious siblings. Most likely, she busied herself thinking about Nelly, Britney, Katy and Kelly or whatever their names are. Or maybe she was too old already and had outgrown her taste for them, and she dreamed of being the second female president—after Hillary, of course.

Her normal physical examination reassured all of us, and her blood counts could not have been better, to the delight of her mother. See you next month, we said—oh how prematurely!

Less than twenty-four hours later she returned, looking quite ill this time. She walked bent forward, her hands pressed against the lower right side of her belly. She had skipped breakfast because looking at food, let alone eating it, made her nauseous. When I examined her later that morning, even light pressure on her abdomen made her squirm in pain. A negative pregnancy test and normal urine and blood work did not allow for a quick diagnosis. My first impression was that Ashley had appendicitis, but that was impossible because she had had an appendectomy seven years earlier.

The specter of recurrent cancer looms large beneath the surface of almost any symptom of these patients, as innocent or short-lived as these symptoms may be. Lymphoma can recur in the uterus or in the ovaries, although these are rare events.

"Rare things are rare" is an old dictum in medicine. Wisdom validated by time. I used to believe it when several of my teachers stated this with full conviction and not a shadow of doubt, but I've long entertained doubts. Rare things keep popping up in front of my eyes with eerie frequency. In my experience, that wisdom, if you want to call it that, is as debunked as the walking, quacking duck I mentioned before.

In Ashley's case, an ultrasound showed a big mass where the ovary should have been. These findings demanded a skillful surgeon.

Dr. Thurgood took one look at Ashley and another at the ultrasound before he rushed her off into the operating room. He and her family were relieved when he called me the next morning. Surrounding the ovary he found an inflammatory lesion he first spelled out as "a mass" and then as "a mess", without any evidence of lymphoma or other cancer. That much became apparent after a preliminary pathologic examination. Thurgood suspected endometriosis. In this disorder, cells lining the inner wall of the uterus migrate into the wrong places and cover the outside of the female organs and the intestines. Her uneventful recovery allowed her to go home on the third day.

Two weeks later came a second call. "We got the final pathology back." Thurgood paused for suspense.

"And?"

"You won't believe it."

"What?" I was getting impatient.

"It's a vegetable," he said.

"What do you mean, a vegetable?"

"She had a vegetable inside her Fallopian tube."

"You are joking, aren't you?"

"No."

I reacted confused, wondering whether he was serious or toying with me. "What kind of a vegetable?"

"Oh, a carrot or cauliflower. Broccoli probably."

"Broccoli?"

"I didn't believe it either, but we sent it out for a second opinion. They confirmed it. You wanna see the photos?"

They confirmed the abstruse diagnosis. You bet I wanted to see them. I showed them to one of our infectious disease colleagues.

"We found this in the pelvis of one of our patients," I said, volunteering no further information. He turned the photos around a few times.

"Looks like a worm, all twisted. What is it?"

"It's a vegetable."

"What?"

"A vegetable."

"You are pulling my leg, aren't you?"

At that moment I remembered what I admittedly had completely forgotten about. During the initial therapy for her lymphoma years ago, Ashley fell violently ill. She developed high fevers, and within a period of hours her abdomen swelled up. She went into shock and required a breathing machine in the intensive care unit for almost a month before she recovered.

Her diagnosis carried a most unpronounceable name, a name, which is derived from the Greek language. No corresponding English term exists: typhlitis, a condition of severe inflammation of the bowel wall we see almost exclusively after aggressive chemotherapy. Interestingly, from the perspective of her later "vegetable illness", she never required surgery. Her bowels may have ruptured and spilled their contents into her belly cavity before they closed spontaneously. Her Fallopian tube could then have captured a vegetable piece in the same way it receives an egg from the ovary before guiding it to the uterus. The tube could have become obstructed and infected. Alternatively, a fistula, an artificial connection, could have developed temporarily between the tube and the adjacent bowel, trapping the vegetable piece inside.

Ashley is well now and free of lymphoma. She still eats her vegetables. The next time you are at the local checkout counter and read unusual stories, think twice before you shake your head and discard them as ridiculous and impossible.

EIGHT

FRIED RICE

I see from my house by the side of the road,
By the side of the highway of life,
The men who press with the ardor of hope,
The men who are faint with the strife.
But I turn not away from their smiles nor tears,
Both parts of an infinite plan-
Let me live in a house by the side of the road
And be a friend to man.

SAM WALTER FOSS, THE HOUSE BY THE SIDE OF THE ROAD

Elephants, hurtling across the sky. I vividly remember these opening words from a newspaper article on animals making their way across the Atlantic en route from Africa to the local zoo. That story ultimately culminated in a whole book called "Zoo stories". Elephants! Hurtling! Quite an image.

Not only pachyderms find themselves guests of the aviation industry. Airplanes commonly carry people and luggage, but they also transport blueberries from Chile, oranges from Israel and flowers from Kenya. Stranger things come to mind, though, like human body parts. A friend of mine transported human placentas from Peru for medical and pharmaceutical research purposes. But now I want to describe another airborne transport of life-saving human tissue, a process that continues to grow world-wide, and for that purpose I need the help of one of my little friends named Cho, who came to the United States on a plane all the way from Korea.

The first time I set foot on this amazing country, someone gave me a precious gift, a copy of the American Declaration of Independence. I have cherished it for decades, and I still have it today. It is one of the greatest documents mankind has ever conceived. I have read and studied it with great admiration for those individuals who put this nation on sound footing for a challenging future. "All men are created equal" resounds through the ages, but there is no question in my mind that Cho was created to be different—and that is not always a disadvantage.

The Boeing 747 landed in Madrid at seven o'clock in the morning, local time. By eight forty, Jeremy Buckner, American, courier of delicate cargo and importer of human tissue, was airborne again and on his way to Barcelona. He carried with him enough pesetas for the two taxi rides and a quick lunch and wasted no time at the currency exchange counter. Assuming everything went as planned, he would pick up his delivery, catch the twelve-fifty flight back to Madrid and make the next connection to Dulles International at three. As long as the airport security people did not give him a hard time, snoop through his papers and insist on inspecting the package at great length, he would be back in the States within less than twenty-four hours. He had to worry more about his own countrymen than the Spaniards. Europeans could not have cared less what he took out of their countries. The Immigration and

Naturalization officials, conversely, left no stone unturned to find out what he brought into his own country.

What a shame he could not spend more time in Spain. Andalusia had always been a dream of his, especially the Alhambra in Granada. Next time, he would have saved up enough money so he could stay for at least a week before his next transport.

Buckner flagged down a taxi at the airport in Barcelona, showed his papers to the driver and made the thirty-minute ride to his destination without problems. A young lady in the Department of Stem Cell Transplantation took him to the back of the office building and into the cold storage room.

"You came four, five months ago, didn't you?" she asked.

"Sure did. I remember you."

"How long will you be travelling this time?" she asked in fluent English, albeit with a sweet accent.

"Twenty-six hours all together." He yawned and scratched the stubble on his chin. "I wish I could spend a few days here. Not with this package, though."

She nodded. "I guess you can't let this stand around anywhere, can you?"

"Not a chance."

"I always wanted to ask: How much do they pay for this in your country?"

"Twenty-five thousand bucks."

"Bucks?"

"Dollars."

She blew out air in between her teeth. "Too bad you can't keep that for yourself. We could split it," she added with a grin. "Crazy how much money for something people throw into the garbage."

Buckner laughed. "Hadn't thought about it that way, but yeah. Sure is expensive garbage."

"Do they tell you who's going to get it?"

"Some kid, that's all I know."

She finished packing the cooler and checked everything one more time before he signed the papers.

"You are set then?" she asked.

"All set! Got to make sure I won't miss the flight back to Madrid at twelve-fifty."

"Good luck. For you and for your little guy."

"Thanks. I'll see you in a few weeks or months, if I'm still doing this job." Quite a lucrative business, he thought in the taxi on his way back to the airport. Twenty-five thousand dollars for a package of human tissue.

The security people in the airport did not ask questions when he explained the purpose of his travel and why he could not put the cooler through the x-ray machine. One of the agents glanced at his papers, gave the cooler a cursory examination and allowed him to pass. During the flight to Madrid, he kept the cooler in between his feet. He even took it into the restroom in the plane—no way could he afford to lose this baby. Things went equally well at the Madrid airport. Eight and a half hours later, he stepped back on American soil, where the cooler raised suspicion enough to force him to almost miss the connecting flight to Tampa, but he muddled through as he always did.

Cho slept peacefully when Buckner delivered the package. He did not wake up when his night nurse hung the thawed package on a pole above his head and let it run through an intravenous tube straight into his bloodstream. Stem cells, whether they derive from cord blood or from bone marrow, will travel to the patient's marrow spaces, settle there and start producing a new set of blood cells that guarantee long-term survival. One human's garbage was now to become another's source of life, proving once again that God's creativity and sense of humor are unlimited.

Not only did Cho stand out amidst the white, black and Hispanic populations in Florida, but even fellow Koreans easily recognized him as uniquely different. Slanted eyes could have been attributed to his race. Delicate features, a tiny frame and bronze-gray skin, on the other hand, set him apart from his parents and his brother. A broad-bridged nose centered in a bird-like face while large, protruding ears gave his expression a degree of mischievousness. Despite malformed thumbs, Cho became a master of the video game, and nobody beat him on his turf.

Cho had Fanconi anemia, a disorder that in most patients leads to failure of the bone marrow within the first five to ten years of life. The numbers of all blood cells decrease over time, and patients succumb to infection and hemorrhage or face the risk of developing leukemia at a later stage. Bone marrow transplantation is the only potential cure.

Unbeknownst to Cho, the transfusion in progress promised to restore his health, although it would not alter his appearance. An intensive search revealed no suitable marrow donor in his family or in the American registries, and his only brother appeared to be too mismatched to be considered a safe alternative. The placenta or afterbirth cord blood of a baby in Barcelona, in contrast, provided almost perfectly matched marrow-derived stem cells. Cho had already completed his chemotherapy and radiation treatment when Buckner brought the cord blood from Spain. Recovery of his normal white and red blood cells as well as platelets should, within a few weeks, signal the successful growth of his new marrow.

Three weeks into his course, Cho looked healthy, but his body had rejected the stem cells. Empty spaces filled the marrow. Either the transatlantic flight had damaged the cord blood, or more likely, Cho's immune system had survived strong enough despite the treatment before the infusion to fight off the baby stem cells. Without his own, now destroyed marrow or that of the donor, Cho could not survive. He needed another transplant, and that needed to come quickly. His mismatched brother provided the best option, although a very risky one.

Cho received high doses of drugs to further suppress his immune system. Days of fevers, chills and nausea led up to the day of his second transplant, an attempt that constituted his last hurrah, his last chance.

After the procedure, another three weeks passed. His blood counts remained dangerously low and his marrow empty. The second transplant failed as miserably as the first.

Cho's only chance, if any existed, lay in a third transplant and a second round of chemotherapy and radiation similar to the treatment he had received prior to the first attempt. In most peoples' assessment he would die from complications of such therapy before he could ever show a response—if he did not reject that third transplant as well.

A trusted colleague in another transplant center listened to my description of the desperate scenario.

"Treatment or no treatment, I'm afraid he won't survive very long," I told her over the telephone. "Have you ever encountered a similar situation?"

"The proverbial rock and the hard place. He probably won't do well, but what other option do you have?"

"You tell me."

"We took care of a kid like him, a couple of years ago. We transplanted him four times. He got chemo and radiation first. After that, two rounds of immunosuppressive therapy. The marrow never took. Before the fourth stem cell infusion, we bit the bullet and gave him chemo and radiation all over."

"Same doses as before the first transplant?"

"Pretty much the same thing. He did fine."

"Amazing. No toxicities?"

"No. He did surprisingly well."

"I guess we have no choice but to try. Koreans are tough." I thought I'd already mentioned Cho's ethnicity when I first described the transplant course, but my colleague apparently hadn't heard me say it.

"Did you say Korean?" she blurted out excitedly.

"Yes. Why?"

"That's weird. Our patient came from Korea also. And there's a third one in New York. Those are the only ones I know who received a transplant from a mismatched, unrelated donor. I don't think they've done those kinds of transplants in Korea yet for this disease. New data suggest Koreans have a different subtype of Fanconi anemia. They are more resistant." She mentioned ongoing research in the field.

"I guess we have no choice but to try, do we?"

"Go for it. Let me know what happens."

Cho's parents and his brother were willing to give Cho one last chance. Despite our fears for the worst, Cho did not develop organ damage. Instead, seventeen days after the third transplant, his white blood cells began to increase, then his red cells and platelets. He experienced no complications, despite his brother's mismatch, and we could send him home to his family with great hope that he would do well. I lost track of him but years later we met elsewhere. Cho was healthy, in school and back at his video game.

Whenever I read about North Koreans and their suffering, I think about Cho, and I realize how tough people from this Far Eastern peninsula are. His mother is a great cook, and I have been a beneficiary of her awesome fried rice and dumplings. I have the surreal image in my mind of her feeding the entire northern half of her divided nation. The opening ceremonies of the Olympics in Sydney gave me great solace when North and South Koreans walked into the stadium together under a single flag. And the hope that in our lifetime one nation may still find its reunion under one flag, with fried rice for all, still remains.

NINE

ONE GIANT STEP

We are the miracles that God made
To taste the bitter fruit of time

BEN OKRI, AN AFRICAN ELEGY: POEMS

———————————————

For the sad old earth must borrow its mirth
But has trouble enough of its own

...one by one we must all file on
Through the narrow isles of pain

ELLA WHEELER WILCOX, SOLITUDE

What good is a leg? Have you ever wondered? Few people bother to contemplate the many parts of their bodies, unless they stop functioning properly. A leg serves many purposes. One can have a leg up or no leg to stand on. One can win or lose the last leg of a race or eat a delicious leg of lamb. Without a leg, one cannot stroll alongside one's girlfriend, take her down the aisle or dance at one's wedding.

Sir Edmund Hillary would not have climbed Mount Everest, and Mikhail Baryshnikov could not have enchanted audiences with his phenomenal strides on the stage. Neither would Neil Armstrong have made his giant step for mankind, nor Bob Beamon his jump of the last century.

Legs can exert a mysterious attraction. Rodin's Thinker amazes me with his strong and muscular thighs. In striking contrast, the spindly limbs of Giacometti's sculptures provoke surprise if not disapproval. The limp lower extremities depicted in the Pieta elicit sorrow. Raphael's exquisite painting of Michelangelo's gout-ravaged legs in the School of Athens creates admiration.

Most people value their legs and want to keep them at all cost, naturally. But not all do. One remarkable young man you will read about shortly certainly did not. The three boys in this chapter all suffered from cancerous tumors of their thigh bones. How exactly do children and teenagers deal with life-threatening illness? No single answer does justice to the wide range of responses from young people who are faced with extreme adversity.

———————————

Smack in the middle of the empty front room stands a leg—a whole leg. If the ghoulish, macabre sight does not stop you frozen in your tracks, you might notice it is a left leg. It has a life of its own, and worse, nobody is around to claim it.

Imagine you have barely left behind the silly, inconsequential dreams of last night. You are not ready to begin a new day. Suppose your mind has wandered off, drifting away like puffed-up clouds in the sky. Envision you open a clinic door through which you have entered year after year, and walk into a room where every nook and cranny is familiar. You expect to be alone, yet the room is not empty. This eerily independent leg commands your complete attention.

A quick succession of thoughts shoots through my mind. *What on earth does this mean? Who would leave a leg? What if anybody sees...?*

Bewilderment gives way to joy, and a broad smile follows. Dan is here; it must be him. Others might have difficulty finding their glasses or their keys, and then they would be forced to search for a while to get them back. Only Dan would leave his artificial leg somewhere—anywhere—and immediately forget what he did with it.

The leg itself does not bother me much. I am, however, concerned about a new family arriving in the office. By the time of their first visit at a specialist's office, children and their parents alike are typically worried or afraid. A lone leg in the middle of the waiting room will hardly calm a mother's anxiety about a serious illness. Moreover, a child's magical thinking can lead to the wildest, scariest ideas so far removed from reality that no parent could fathom them. Needless to say, we do not want any spare body parts lying around..

As I turn away to go find the leg's missing owner, I think how, in light of Dan's extraordinary journey, this lone leg represents a flagpole of perseverance and a beacon of hope and courage. It is not an admission of defeat or acceptance of failure.

Leaving the leg where I found it, I enter the clinic, where Dan's mother is engaged in a conversation with the receptionist. She acknowledges me with a brief nod, then resumes the sentence she left hanging in the air. I smile back, eager not to interrupt, and walk to the treatment rooms.

Dan is already sitting on an examination table. His crutches lean against the wall while his right leg dangles innocently down the table. He kicks the space in front of him with his foot as if he wants to fire off a few imaginary soccer balls. Dan smiles and this already makes my day. Neither his face nor his life has room for sorrow, self-pity or resignation. Quite to the contrary, his smile is infectious.

"Where's your leg?" Maintaining composure opposite Dan's bedazzled countenance is difficult. Dan glances down his body but sees only his remaining extremity before he realizes I'm not talking about his right leg. In surprise, he scans the room to find the other but notices only his crutches.

"Oh…" he says with the most disarming expression. He scratches the back of his head and with a puzzled look, he adds, "I think I left it in the waiting room. You want me to get it?"

How do I respond to that? *Yes, I need to check out that artificial leg of yours and make sure it's OK? Or, you better get it before someone steals it?*

Dan cannot hobble around on his crutches and carry the leg in his hands at the same time. I need to examine the stump of the thigh, an impossible task when the leg is attached to it.

"Well, no. I might as well check you out since you're already up on the table. Next time, please don't leave it out in the clinic like that! Do you have any idea what people might think if they came for the first time and saw your leg in the middle of the room?"

"I don' know," Dan mumbles.

Of course he does! "Come on, Dan!" I stretch out his name to twice its normal length to give more weight to my fake disapproval.

Dan tilts his head sideways as if to convince me he might not have the slightest idea. "Nothin', maybe…"

I give him my stern, reproachful look, the harshest I can bring forth. It is hard not to burst out laughing.

"Scared, maybe," Dan adds quietly.

"I would think so. You remember when you first showed up here?"

"Yeah."

Enough of a sermon; I do not need to press the issue any further. "How are you doing anyway?"

"He's doing great," his mother chimes in before Dan can answer. I had not noticed her enter. She's correct, of course. Anybody who leaves his prosthesis in the waiting room and his mother at the reception desk has adjusted well. If Dan had been doing poorly, his mother would have been in the exam room with him from the moment they got to the clinic. Seeing her engaged in a friendly conversation with the receptionist had already convinced me everything was in order.

Indeed, Dan is doing well. He is only twelve years old, but things looked different a year ago. He and his family, I'm certain, won't ever forget that darkest moment in their lives when they discovered that osteosarcoma, a cancerous tumor of his thighbone, snuck up on him out of nowhere. The mass above the knee grew to the size of a grapefruit and caused pain and deformity, leaving doctors little choice. Any surgery less radical than amputation would have threatened Dan's chances for survival and cure.

Surgery, nevertheless, required back-up intervention on a large scale. Despite the horrible operation he endured, the prognosis with this treatment alone would have been dismal. Over eighty percent of children like Dan experience spread of the disease to the lungs or to other bones, and ultimately succumb to their cancer unless they receive additional treatment. The technical term is chemotherapy; however, we often use the word "medicines" as a neutral expression to explain this concept in a gentle way. This rather deceptive euphemism misses the heart of the matter. "Controlled poisoning" is a more honest term.

Yet, who wants to have his child undergo controlled poisoning? Convincing patients and parents alike that this additional therapy is in the child's best interest is time-consuming. "*Without* surgery," a famous surgeon stated decades ago at a cancer conference, "they all die. *With* surgery, they all die. We might as well conclude this meeting with a prayer."

Fortunately, other more effective options have come along over the last twenty to thirty years. Not that prayer is wrong or inappropriate—far from it. Prayer, research proves, saves lives.

Dan has recently completed all therapy. The stump of the thigh shows no signs of recurrent disease, and the healthy appearance of the skin suggests the prosthesis fits well. Dan will undergo x-rays and CAT scans of his lungs and the remnant of his leg for years to come. He will do fine, for he has always proven the attitude of can-do and the fighting spirit to get him through this ordeal. The prosthesis is a different story. Dan is bound to lose it. He will hobble around, asking everyone in sight whether they have seen his leg, blissfully oblivious to the bewilderment or horror in their faces.

Dan's cancer therapy involved three drugs, all of which have serious, occasionally life-threatening side effects. I developed a deep respect for these drugs when I took care of my first cancer patient. The confession that I was clueless at that time would be an understatement.

Joey carried seventeen years under his belt and had Dan's type of bone tumor. Back then I was only ten years older than Joey, and barely three months into my training in pediatrics. The responsibility to monitor Joey's therapy frightened me quite a bit. Joey's medical orders included a very high dose of Methotrexate, a drug designed to deplete the tumor cells of a vitally important nutrient. Twenty-four hours after the start of the therapy, an antidote needed to be injected to protect the normal tissues from the toxic effects of the drug. The amount of this antidote depended on the drug levels in Joey's blood. Getting the dosage wrong was simply not an option.

Joey's attending physician, Dr. Myra, owned a voice as deep and dark as a mineshaft—in fact so deep that people who talked to her on the telephone for the first time invariably thought she was a man. Rumors circulated that she drank nothing but bear's milk the first few years of her life. I knew of her but I had never met her.

Dr. Myra asserted in staccato sentences that the first drug level due in the middle of the night demanded my utmost attention. Before I could go to sleep, my job required that I find out whether the dose of the antidote needed adjustment.

"You better check that level or I'll rip your head off," she said bluntly. Her intimidating voice left no room for doubt or compromise.

I feared the worst, for Joey and for myself. Joey, on the other hand, spent a peaceful night. My head did remain attached for the duration of the clinical rotation. Beyond a tough outer shell, I learned quickly, Dr. Myra possessed a heart of gold and an unrivaled passion for the children in her care. She truly looked after them like a Mama Bear, and woe befalls the one who stands between a mama bear and her cubs.

Michael was only ten years old when he gave up one of his legs voluntarily, although he could have undergone a limb-saving type of surgery. He loved life. More than anything else, he loved to play sports—soccer, football and baseball, anything that involved kicking, throwing or batting. X-rays revealed a bone tumor in his thigh. He was a good candidate for the type of surgery that could have spared his leg and still helped cure his cancer.

Once chemotherapy shrinks the tumor, surgeons remove the cancerous part of the bone and implant a cadaver bone or an artificial joint to replace it. Months of physical therapy follow. The procedure renders the extremity far more vulnerable to injury than a healthy limb, and it precludes participation in most sports. Michael could not bear to even consider this possibility. He adamantly defended his decision that he wanted an amputation. His distraught parents could not understand his refusal to save his leg. Anyone in his sound mind, they felt, would have insisted on salvage of the leg if possible under almost any circumstance.

Is a ten-year-old boy competent to make a decision of this magnitude? Was removal of the leg ethical if a far less mutilating alternative existed? A child psychiatrist examined Michael and found him responsible beyond his age, and the hospital chaplain admitted to being highly impressed by Michael's maturity. Nothing changed the boy's mind. Michael made his decision and in the end, everyone supported him. Six weeks after surgery, he returned to the field. He was still a bit clumsy and unsteady, adjusting to his preliminary prosthesis but ready to play.

He would not have fought and survived his disease, had people not listened to him and allowed him to live his life on his own terms.

As opposed to Dan, Michael won't leave his prosthesis out of his sight and risk losing it even for a blink of an eye. The likelihood he might not be able to join the guys on the ball field would be far too big.

Andy had almost reached adulthood. Like Michael, he loved football. He had already become a star athlete on his high school football team. He was a magnificent wide receiver and had good reason to expect a college scholarship. Nothing stood between him and a promising future—nothing except a single game. He broke his thighbone, which is one of the strongest in the human body. Despite its resilience, a tackle or a collision between players in fierce competition can break this bone.

Andy did not tell anyone of the subtle pain he had been experiencing before the game. Growing pains, muscle fatigue, a strain, hard practice—he couldn't tell what might have started his symptoms. But for a tough man like him, slowing down let alone bench-warming during a game, was simply out of the question.

When an emergency room physician finally obtained an x-ray, any lay person could have diagnosed the fracture. Nobody noticed a second, far less conspicuous irregularity until after disaster struck. Hindsight is easy when someone else shoves your nose on the abnormality you are supposed to notice.

An orthopedic surgeon inserted a rod into the soft core of Andy's thighbone from the hip through the fracture site down to the knee. A cast gave additional support. In a month or two, he asserted confidently, the bone would heal and regain its original strength. He would then take off the cast and remove the rod.

Andy experienced pain for weeks. Given the magnitude of the fracture, the family thought that the pain Andy experienced was normal. Eventually, his leg ought to feel better, and he could not wait to play again. But instead of subsiding, the pain became unbearable. Another x-ray revealed that the fracture had not healed—far from it. A mass at the fracture site had destroyed the bone, and a biopsy confirmed cancer. By then, Andy's disease had spread throughout his thigh and to his skin, making an amputation of the entire leg the sole remaining option.

Telling him the truth came at a stiff price. If Andy did not hate us, he certainly hated everything we said. For him, the message and the messenger were one and the same. Andy saw life disintegrate and evaporate in front of his eyes. Playing football turned into an illusion, as his hopes for a scholarship vanished. College became a reality only in his dreams. He counted his future in months, not years, and he did not want to live a miserable life. He may not have wanted to live at all.

One thing remained certain: without the amputation, Andy would not have survived. On a positive note, his disease had not spread to other parts of his body. Freedom from metastases allowed for a reasonable start, but Andy wanted to hear none of this.

Many doctors, nurses and other caregivers got involved in Andy's care. At first, he ignored or even hated them all. He needed time. Slowly but surely, he followed the path most cancer patients walk. Disbelief, anger, frustration, bargaining, acceptance (as Elisabeth Kübler-Ross, the Swiss-American psychiatrist identified in her ground-breaking studies) and, ultimately, the resolution to fight and survive were all steps he took at his own pace.

Months later, Andy and I played basketball on the roof garden of the hospital. He knew he would never play the competitive football he had always dreamed of, the game that promised to make him famous. By now, however, he had become a star of a different kind. He served as a big brother of sorts for many of the younger children on the cancer ward who looked up to him with admiration and thrived on his words of encouragement. Often they followed him across the halls and mimicked him using his IV pole as a make-believe skateboard. Only somebody like Andy who had faced that desperate trial himself could understand what they were going through, and find the right words to lift them up.

Years after therapy, Andy is healed from his tumor and taking pre-med courses in college with a hefty scholarship to his credit. He will be a fine and compassionate doctor someday.

TEN

CORRECT MISDIAGNOSES

Build today, then, strong and sure,
With a firm and ample base;
And ascending and secure
Shall tomorrow find its place.

HENRY WADSWORTH LONGFELLOW, THE BUILDERS

If I can stop one heart from breaking,
I shall not live in vain:
If I can ease one life from aching,
Or cool one pain

EMILY DICKINSON, NOT IN VAIN

I remember a little boy with prolonged fevers, who suffered from a ruptured appendix that required weeks of intravenous antibiotics and complicated surgery thereafter. For quite a while, every one of his doctors focused on subtle abnormalities in CAT scans of the boy's abdomen, which had resulted from the appendicitis surgery, and all missed the big tumor in his heart that no one anticipated or looked for.

Another example that fits this bill of diagnostic blindness is a sixteen-year-old young man with sickle cell anemia, who developed fevers after the removal of his gall bladder. He was black, and his caregivers labeled him an African American. I assume he did not speak much because he did not feel good, or he acted shy, but certainly no one realized that his English sounded a bit unusual. All of us missed the fact that he was African all right, but not American. He'd recently emigrated from Nigeria and brought malaria with him from home.

Excellent vision, stellar hearing and even a sharp mind do not always protect us from missing the forest for the trees. Doctors are human. Like most people, they only see and search for things they already have on their minds. All too often, they subconsciously ignore other possibilities, and miss what does not fit on their self-imposed radar screen.

———————————

Harsh light, cold silver-metal instruments, and green scrubs made for an inhospitable environment. The threatening surroundings notwithstanding, Malcolm knew he had committed to the right thing. It did not take much effort on his parents' part to convince him to go to the hospital. Too many years had passed for him to remember his last operation and procedures. Yet when Malcolm's father recounted the misery of his son's early life, Malcolm could have reported it himself. He knew the minutest detail for his parents and grandparents had told the story a thousand times.

He walked down the long corridor, an ostensibly simple accomplishment for which he owed his sister a huge debt. Malcolm knew there was no alternative, but even if another option existed, he would have insisted that he be allowed to step up to the plate.

An hour later, he said good-bye to his parents. A nurse wheeled him into the operating room. The thought of surgery did not bother him despite his perfect health. Soon, the anesthesia gas forced him into a deep, relaxing sleep. Waking up two hours later, he knew he was giving life, precious life. He had kept his part in the bargain; he had paid her back.

Malcolm saw the light of the world two years before his sister Marie's birth. He did not learn to walk despite surgery and long-standing physical therapy, causing his parents to worry whether he ever would. Malcolm was born with the birth defect known as spina bifida. The spinal column in his lower back did not close completely, and that defect led to injury of the nerves to his legs.

Marie, on the other hand, started to pull herself to a stand at the age of eight months. She took her first unassisted steps at ten and a half months, and Malcolm's intrigued eyes followed her across the room. On his own he could not imitate her, however much he wanted to do the things she performed so effortlessly in front of him.

Marie discovered her independence and needed a playmate. Malcolm, her only option, did not qualify in his immobile condition. She found his impairment intolerable but intuitively knew she could get him to learn what she mastered so quickly. Marie succeeded where surgery and physical therapy had failed. Within half a year, Malcolm walked. The two were inseparable from then on.

When Marie turned nine years old, her parents noticed how pale and easily fatigued she was. Her pediatrician diagnosed anemia but did not like the way she looked, so he referred her for an evaluation. Her skin showed a grayish tinge. Dark rings sat underneath sunken eyes, and her movements looked hesitant. Her mother reported a recent fever accompanied by a pink, lacy skin rash and aches in Marie's elbows and knees. These latter symptoms resolved on their own, suggesting the possibility of a harmless childhood illness. A parvovirus infection, also known as Fifth Disease, could explain her symptoms and her low red blood cells.

I was concerned enough because of the way she looked to perform a bone marrow test to rule out leukemia. Subtle changes of the red cells led me to believe that a viral infection had to be responsible. A simple blood test later confirmed a parvovirus infection, which required no further intervention or treatment. I instructed the nurses to throw away the two extra teaspoons of bone marrow I had obtained for special tests in case leukemia had raised its ugly head. One specimen landed in the trash can. The other, however, inadvertently found its way to the Department of Genetics when a laboratory technician took a sample. Marie went home with the expectation that she would be just fine.

Within ten days, the results of chromosome studies surfaced unexpectedly. Marie's marrow cells contained forty-seven rather than the usual forty-six chromosomes humans carry in each normal cell. The extra chromosome indicated an aggressive leukemia. Underneath the simple infection, a second, life-threatening illness lurked, which became apparent only through the inadvertent, canceled test. We had correctly misdiagnosed our little patient.

A repeat marrow test revealed profoundly different, highly aggressive changes unrelated to the parvovirus infection. Her bone marrow cancer came with a prognosis that was even worse than that of a "normal" leukemia, and conventional chemotherapy could not cure this disease.

From one moment to the next, Marie's family faced not only the prospects of a deadly disorder but also the need for a marrow transplant as the sole option. She had only one sibling; therefore chances of us finding a suitable donor in the family were hardly better than twenty-five percent.

All eyes turned to Malcolm who had quietly followed the conversation from a chair in the corner of the room.

By the time Malcolm entered the operating room, Marie had already completed eight days of chemotherapy that destroyed her cancer in addition to her few remaining normal marrow and immune cells. She would die without her brother's help, but he came through for her when it counted. Tissue typing showed him to be a perfect match, and he grew plenty of healthy marrow in his hips to spare for his sister, whom she owed so much.

"You can't compete in the Olympics; you know that, don't you?" I asked Marie after her discharge from the hospital. Only her sparse hair suggested her recent ordeal. The thought of participating in the Olympics apparently never occurred to her, but when I categorically excluded her from ever participating without a good reason, she became upset.

"Why not?" she asked angrily.

"You may have to get a blood test. Then they'd find out you were cheating."

"No, I wouldn't be cheating," Marie answered with a stern voice.

"Yes, you would."

"No, I wouldn't."

"They'd find out you were a man."

"Nu-uh!"

"I've got proof," I pronounced with a stern look.

Marie became suspicious. Her "No, you don't" came markedly softer than her prior denial of wrongdoing.

"You wanna see?" By now, her curiosity forced her to let down her guard.

"What kind of chromosomes do women have?" I asked mischievously.

"I don't know."

"46, including two X's."

Marie looked towards her mother. "It's true," her mother confirmed with a serious nod.

"And men?" I continued.

"I don't know," Marie answered in frustration.

"46, one X, one Y."

Her mother shook her head in agreement.

"Here, look at this." I held the computer print-out with the chromosome analysis of her blood cells after the transplant under her nose. "See, everyone has an X and a Y. All male cells. Marie, you are cheating. You are a man. Come on, admit it."

One of the secretaries in our office who was unfamiliar with marrow transplant procedures had been listening in to the conversation. She had grown particularly fond of Marie and her family. "Let me see," she budged in. I let her look at the test result.

"Oh my God," she responded, alarmed. "Are you sure?"

Marie panicked, turning to her only resort. "Mom!"

"Oh Honey, that's wonderful."

Marie did not quite get the drift, but at least the lack of concern in her mother's response comforted her a bit.

"It's only the blood cells, Honey, not the rest of your body. They are Malcolm's. You have a whole new bone marrow. Of course, you are not a boy."

Marie gave me a stern look of disapproval and disgust. "Liar," she said and walked out of the room.

Years later, Marie is a healthy and beautiful young woman. I think she has forgiven me. I promised not be so mean again, to her or anyone else.

———————

If I told you about a young kid, whose diagnosis of a life-threatening illness obscured an even more lethal disease that might have been curable had it been picked up sooner, you would likely call this a horrible, depressing story. You would ask me how anyone can—or would want to—possibly manage to take care of children under such circumstances.

All I can think of in answering that question is to pose a counter question. How can one not take care of a child like this, one of the most vulnerable the Lord could ever put in one's way. It is worth it to know that one has made a difference, that one has been allowed to be a witness to another's life, to have loved and cried together, and realized that this earthly existence never signifies the end of the entire story. I took care of a little friend named Paul, and his story is a perfect example. I feel I need to honor him, and the only way I know how to do that is by leaving behind an ever-so-small literary monument to his oh-so-short walk here on earth with us.

For as far back as Paul could think, One Hundred Acre Wood stood out as his favorite place. In case you don't remember, Winnie-the-Pooh lived in the One Hundred Acre Wood. In this beautiful world, he hummed proudly to himself, searching for honey and the mysterious Woozle.

Paul knew everything about Piglet assisting Pooh in trapping a Heffalump in a Very Deep Pit, near Six Pine Trees. Eeyore's loss of his tail saddened him, though he rejoiced when Pooh found a new one. Kanga, Baby Roo and Rabbit were all old acquaintances. Yet Paul loved none of Christopher Robin's many friends more than he loved Tigger.

The striped, orange tiger bounced and leaped effortlessly through the One Hundred Acre Wood as if his skinny legs were made of metal coils. The ability to jump into action at the spur of a moment made Tigger special. Not a day passed that Paul did not take his Tigger puppet along, regardless of where he needed to go. The two remained inseparable, which earned Paul the nickname "Tiggerman."

Paul never explained why he thought Tigger was so much more important or special than the other characters in the Winnie-the-Pooh stories. He held a dark secret no one knew about, not even his parents: Tigger could jump and leap. Paul, who had turned five years old a few months earlier, could not.

One day Paul complained of pain in his hip and dragged his turned-out leg behind him. His parents thought he might have fallen out of his bunk bed or pulled a muscle and took him to his pediatrician when the pain did not improve. She asked a few simple questions and took a careful look at her patient. What she heard and saw alarmed her. Paul could not climb a short set of stairs unless he pulled himself up along the railing. He used his arms to push his trunk off his thighs to raise himself off the floor. His legs were even weaker than his arms. A nerve specialist shared her suspicions. Molecular analysis confirmed the diagnosis of Duchenne muscular dystrophy. The disease leads to progressive muscle weakness. It is incurable. By the age of twenty years, most patients are wheel chair-bound, and they die because they cannot muster the strength to breathe.

His parents found the devastating diagnosis hard to accept but decided to give Paul all the love and care they could possibly bestow upon him. A cure, they hoped, or at least an effective therapy might come along in the next ten or fifteen years before time ran out for him. Intensive physical therapy led to improvement in Paul's discomfort. The pain, however, never completely went away.

Half a year later, he developed a lump in the groin. The suspected hernia turned out to be a solid mass. A surgeon removed the lump, a rock-hard lymph node, which had grown far too big and contained far too many unusual cells. Additional tests showed a highly aggressive muscle tumor spreading beyond the lymph node. Huge lumps already swelled in his pelvis and belly. Paul took months of chemotherapy and radiation in stride. The tumor responded initially but soon recurred. The correct diagnosis of one awful disorder had delayed the discovery of another horrific disease and, perhaps, curative therapy.

Often I would sit on his bed for a little while and learn new stories of Tigger's—and Paul's—life that burst with fantasy and creativity. You may not be able to prescribe chemotherapy or figure out radiation treatments, but you and I and almost everyone else can invest a little bit of time and show care and compassion for someone who is going through hard times. You don't have to worry too much that you might say the wrong thing, hurt this individual's feelings or be the wrong person for the job.

Until the end, Tigger stood by his friend's side and brought joy to Tiggerman. What Paul could not do, he created through his puppet for everyone to see: a creature bouncing and jumping on his belly and his bed that allowed him to live vicariously the life he would never have. When Paul died, Tigger came right along.

I was angry with God. Confused. Disappointed. Frustrated. In the course of Tiggerman's suffering, the why questions came rolling back, until one day this crazy, not particularly biblical image popped into my brain: if justice reigns in heaven and the new earth to come, Paul will be in charge of the fruit trees. Ladders will be abolished, for Tiggerman will leap boundlessly to the highest branches out of reach for everyone else.

Someone will have to tell him to leave the forbidden apples alone. In his exuberance, he will pick them all. There's no guarantee he might not get mankind into trouble a second time around.

I miss little Tiggerman.

ELEVEN

YOU ONLY LIVE TWICE

Doubtful, for a while
Not knowing what to feel or if I understand
Or whether wise or foolish, tardy or too soon.

T.S. Eliot, Poems

Teach me half the gladness
That thy brain must know,
Such harmonious madness
From my lips would flow,
The world should listen then,
As I am listening now.

Percy Bysshe Shelley, To a Skylark

Friends of ours have been serving as missionaries on the Philippine island of Cebu for many years. On their rare furloughs, we have enjoyed their first-hand accounts of a people and culture that are quite foreign to us. Three of their stories I remember well. The first painted a curious and colorful picture of the importance of food and its significance in hospitality. Our friends had been invited to a *five-pig wedding*, a feast so opulent, as evidenced by the number of pigs slaughtered, that there could be no question as to the social prestige and magnanimity of the bride's family. The second was a hilarious account of chickens wandering past worshippers during Sunday church services. The third story dealt with the commonality of death and dying in the community and home setting even young children witness routinely.

Life in Cebu takes place in the open, and so does death because so often it cannot be sanitized, hidden and denied behind the obscuring walls of hospitals and funeral homes.

Conventional wisdom has it that human beings, whether in Cebu or in Florida or anywhere in between, die only once. Time and experience have taught me that this is not always correct. Eternal life on the other hand, I'm convinced, is still a one-time event.

I once met a man from whom I quickly learned an important, unsuspected truth. You only live twice. A thunderbolt shot through me when he told the following story.

At the time, I was serving as the inpatient attending physician on the cancer ward. We had admitted a fourteen-year-old young man who looked pale as a ghost. Changes in his skin color developed so gradually that the father simply did not notice. Only after bruises developed and people asked about the boy's pallor did he realize his son had a serious problem. All his blood cells dropped to dangerously low levels, and his bone marrow nurtured nothing but empty spaces. This condition is known as aplastic anemia. Patients suffer from life-threatening infections and bleeding. Therapy would be prolonged and cumbersome at best but fraught with serious complications, and nobody could guarantee it would succeed in a cure. The social worker involved in his son's case asked the father a simple question to elicit his coping skills.

"Has anything as serious as this ever happened to you or your family?" she wanted to know.

"Never," he answered quickly. After momentary hesitation, he added, unfazed,

"Except once. When I woke up in the morgue."

Now he attracted the social worker's undivided attention. "What do you mean?" she asked, not sure whether she understood correctly.

"There was this guy coming at me. He held a knife in his hand. I think he was gonna cut me open. I sat up real fast and yelled, what are you gonna do to me?! He screamed and threw up his arms; his knife flew through the air. He turned around and ran out of the room."

"What were you doing there?"

"I don't know. They said I was dead."

"Dead?"

"Yeah. I guess I had some kind of an accident or something."

"What did you do?"

"I went home."

No further questions proved necessary. His coping skills were indisputable. Since then his son has lived with ample opportunity to show he is up to par with his father.

If I ever questioned whether one could live twice, one of my friends proved this truth correct beyond a shadow of a doubt.

For months ten-year-old Shelby had been fighting a treacherous illness and was slowly losing ground. For every step forward she took another one or two back. Her leukemia went haywire. Fevers and infections developed, while her liver, spleen and lymph glands swelled up. Ugly blotches covered her skin.

She could not breathe on her own, required a breathing machine and lay in her bed as helplessly as her doctors and nurses stood around her day in and day out.

Bone marrow transplantation might have cured her disease, but we could not find a donor. For a while, aggressive chemotherapy suppressed her illness but it led to more complications. Her kidneys suffered and her liver began to fail. Improvement was unlikely, recovery unfathomable. Her mother wanted everything humanly possible done. In her infinite pain, she could not even consider stopping all therapy and allowing her daughter to die a peaceful death.

One late night, and to no one's surprise, Shelby's heart stood still from one short moment to the next. Her death had been a foregone conclusion. Within seconds the senior intensive care physician and his team started chest compressions to substitute for the failing heart and pump blood around Shelby's limp and lifeless body. Emergency medications to push her heart into action were futile. Metal paddles pressed against her chest delivered an electric shock that made no difference either. Shelby was simply gone.

Penny, her nurse, called the mother to inform her about Shelby's desperate situation. Her mother begged Penny with panic in her voice to not give up on Shelby under any circumstance before she made it to the hospital.

Chest compressions continued. Further medications to stimulate the heart into action failed. A second electric shock bore no results, and a third, fourth and fifth round proved equally fruitless. Shelby showed no response. The nurse compressing her chest became exhausted and another nurse stepped in to relieve her.

"This doesn't make any sense. Where's the mother?" Dr. Gruber bellowed, visibly upset.

"On her way. She said she'd be here in twenty minutes tops. She begged me not to give up on Shelby until she got here," Penny said.

"Twenty minutes? Those are long up! Give her another Epi," he ordered one of the nurses, who drew up into syringes the medications that a fourth nurse then injected into Shelby's intravenous line. Epinephrine forces the heart to beat stronger and faster.

"Another Bicarb and Calcium!"

Dr. Gruber asked the nurse to interrupt the chest compressions so he could look for spontaneous heartbeats. Electrodes connected Shelby's chest to a monitor above the head of her bed. Earlier in the day, the EKG had indicated Shelby's heartbeat with a rhythmic blip a hundred and forty times a minute. Now it remained deadly silent, a flat line being the only thing the team had noticed since the beginning of the resuscitation efforts.

"Keep pumping," Dr. Gruber demanded. Further electric shocks proved futile: a sixth, a seventh, an eighth, a ninth round. "Where's the mother?"

"I don't know," Penny repeated, exasperated. "She said she'd be here as soon as she could. It wouldn't be more than twenty minutes."

"Shock her again." Shelby's body jerked up and then became limp once again.

"Another Epi!"

The team saw no response. Half an hour passed. Eight rounds of medicines and ten electric shocks made no difference whatsoever.

"That's it. I'm calling the code," Dr. Gruber said to indicate the end of the futile efforts. All eyes turned to the monitor. Shelby's heart had ceased beating forever. Instead of blips, a silent, flat line stretched across the screen. Shelby died before her mother got a chance to say farewell.

The room stood empty except for Shelby's bruised body and Penny, who had been responsible for Shelby's care since the evening hours. She had been caring for her for the last ten days. She knew her mother well and realized how distraught she would be, seeing her daughter dead on the bed.

Cleaning up a body is never a light-hearted event, but that work constituted part of Penny's job and she felt a certain reward when her patients looked clean and peaceful. The final moments of a life ebbing away in an intensive care unit are often invariably messy. Although none of what she did after a death changed anything for her patients, such care certainly mattered to their loved ones. It gave dignity to the dead. Full of gentleness, she wiped away the bloody secretions from Shelby's mouth and face.

Preparing to disconnect the electrodes from Shelby's chest, Penny looked through a glass window and noticed the mother approach in the hallway. Penny had sworn she would call immediately if things turned bad during the night. The mother wanted to be present under all circumstances, but Penny had said something earlier in the day about Shelby being reasonably stable. She had not expected anything serious to happen this night. Penny felt guilty. She could not bear the thought of having to face Shelby's mother the moment she realized her daughter had died. At the spur of the moment, she grabbed the electric paddles.

Shelby was dead. Nothing Penny did to her mattered anymore. Another shock might make her mother believe Shelby was still alive, and she could say her good-byes. Penny could make her believe she had arrived in time, and Shelby's mother would cherish forever the memory of having been with her daughter in her final moments. None of these thoughts made sense to Penny when she recapitulated the incident later, but in the heat of the moment, she thought her actions justifiable.

Shelby's mother entered the room the moment Penny jolted Shelby's fragile body for the eleventh time. Shelby had already been dead for a while—not counting half an hour of desperate resuscitation efforts. The electric shock jolted her lifeless body with a loud pang. Shelby's mother cried out at the sight of the limp body and buried her face in her daughter's neck.

Blip.

A single audible blip came from the direction of the monitor behind Penny's back…then a second….then another.

"Oh no," Penny stammered, horrified, but unnoticed by Shelby's mother.

Blip, blip, blip came the sounds from the monitor with rhythmic regularity. The flat line transformed into the rugged, normal pattern that had been missing for the last forty-five minutes.

Penny yelled for help. Out of the blue, Dr. Gruber stood at the foot of Shelby's bed. He had been writing his note to document the event. His eyes wandered from the monitor to Penny, Shelby, her mother and back to the screen.

"What's going on?" His voice cut through the air like a sharp knife. Penny did not want to answer, but terrified she whispered,

"I shocked her."

"You did what?"

"I gave her another electric shock," she muttered.

"This will have consequences. Hook her up to the vent. We need respiratory therapy, STAT. Get a blood gas and chemistries, now," he said, unable to control his anger.

"Did they tell you what happened last night?" Marcia asked when I entered Shelby's room at seven forty-five in the morning. Marcia had taken over Shelby's care at the end of Penny's shift.

"No, what happened?"

Marcia outlined the events of the night, hinting at Penny's emotional turmoil. "I don't know what to do. Dr. Gruber is furious because of what she did."

"Why is he so upset? Because he declared her dead and now Shelby's alive?"

"No, because Shelby is going to be brain damaged. Way too much time passed between the end of the code and the time her heart came back."

"But how could she have known?"

"That's not the point. She got specific orders and she acted against those orders, completely on her own. Who's going to take the responsibility for her now? What if she survives for fifty years, with severe brain damage?"

I didn't know the answer. I don't often run across a dead girl come alive. Instead, I turned to Shelby.

"Hey Shelby, how're you doing?"

Shelby opened her eyes—quite a feat for a brain damaged child. I put two fingers into the palm of her hand. She squeezed them on command. Brain damaged she was not.

Dr. Gruber and one of his colleagues stood in the hall, discussing the case.

"Should have never happened," he barked, letting off steam as I approached him. "She took it on her own, counter to my orders. The kid will survive, maybe, but her brain will be mush."

"Come on, Jim, she didn't know. She did it to help her mom, from what I can tell. How could she have known this would happen? By the way, when I checked her out, she opened her eyes and squeezed my fingers."

"She did?" he asked, visibly shocked. "Well, maybe. I don't believe it."

Shelby's liver did not get better. Her horrendous illness, the long, aggressive therapy and the protracted resuscitation efforts made a meaningful recovery impossible. She could not endure further treatments.

Her mother had her flown to another hospital for investigational therapy. Shortly after she arrived at the new center, her kidneys began to fail, and any further aggressive treatment became out of the question. Her mother lay at Shelby's side in her bed, cradling and comforting her little body when she died again. She lived twice.

TWELVE

SURPRISE, SURPRISE

Outward sunshine, inward joy;
Blessings on thee, barefoot boy!
Oh, for boyhood's painless play,
Sleep that wakes in laughing day,
Health that mocks the doctor's rules,
Knowledge never learned of schools…

JOHN GREENLEAF WHITTIER, THE BAREFOOT BOY

For one hundred and twenty-odd years, my daughter's friend lived as a nameless nobody. He was born around 1880 but the details of his past remained obscure. Some people speculated he might have weathered wars and revolution and witnessed kings and tyrants come and go. Others believed he must have escaped the turmoil of the Twentieth century altogether and instead lived a life in quiet obscurity.

Time did not treat him kindly. He looked tired—his body broken, his voice silenced—and languished without purpose. One day a stranger locked eyes with him and recognized inner beauty shining through a decrepit exterior. Hidden beneath an exhausted physique lay a great potential that awaited discovery. The stranger gave him a nameless life, but it was a new life nonetheless.

Only when Mr. Cello purchased a plane ticket, did he get his name. With that name came the amenities of modern existence: credit cards, frequent flier miles, stale peanuts, pretzels and other scrumptious airline food to munch on.

My daughter started to play the cello at the age of ten, but she quickly outgrew half and three-quarter size instruments. Meeting full-bodied Mr. Cello, she found love at first sight. A luthier had unearthed him at an auction in Boston and brought him to Florida, where he restored him with painstaking attention to form and function. His wooden body's beautiful luster and varnish complemented a stunning, sonorous sound.

Rumor had it, Mr. Cello was English. An English church cello, to be specific. The origin of this rumor remained untraceable, its claim unsubstantiated, and its falsehood uncorrected. Mr. Cello carried a smirk in his eyes and a few chuckles under his ribs. He felt honored, for he considered himself in good company. Edward Elgar, after all, was an Englishman whose elegiac cello concerto stands as one of the most striking of the entire repertoire. Jacqueline du Pre, who also grew up English, made the concerto famous. Playing Elgar thrilled Mr. Cello when he joined forces with the Youth Orchestra in Tampa. Despite his comfort in the circle of British greats, he had known all along he was of a different breed, but he never corrected this falsehood. The truth would catch up with him in due time.

Another flight brought the issue into focus. A vigilant, suspicious airport security officer noticed Mr. Cello in the company of two suspect female individuals. Three airline tickets required more than the two picture identification cards the ladies were able to provide. Homeland security is indeed a serious business not to be trifled with. Mr. Cello could not establish his identity and almost failed to board the plane. He denied any inclination to cause trouble and certainly did not insist on access to the cockpit. The officer, nevertheless, feared the worst. Corelli's *Adagio* or Rachmaninoff's *Vocalise* would lull the pilots into a state of hyper-relaxation before they could activate the autopilot. Sollima's rambunctious *Alone* or Shostakovich's sonata might agitate the pilots into frenzy and seduce them into *Top Gun* aerobatics. Gentle perseverance and persuasion on Mr. Cello's behalf finally allowed him to proceed. Why no one ever grilled him over his endpin—sixteen inches of sharpened iron rod sufficient to make Shish kabob of a bull, not to mention a pilot—remained beyond his comprehension.

In the end, Mr. Cello failed to keep secret the identity he had refused to divulge for so long when he returned to the place of his second birth for a tune-up. A comment on his English heritage elicited immediate correction. Mr. Cello, the luthier alleged, had a German background. How could he tell, I asked, and royally embarrassed myself. Did they not all look the same? The question prompted the luthier's scorn. Only an ignoramus could ask that! Derision gave way to grace. He kindly explained the differences in the construction of the body, neck, peg box and scroll of cellos of diverse provenience. Catalogs of instruments from across Europe supported his assertion.

Where in Germany, I wanted to know? Mr. Cello came from a small town my daughter and I allegedly would have never heard of. After repeated questions, the luthier reluctantly volunteered the answer: Markneukirchen in Saxony. The small city close to the Czech Republic harbors one of the two major production centers of string instruments in the country.

The largest business in town in the late eighteen hundreds belonged to a certain Woldemar Schuster. By all accounts, Woldemar was a remarkable man. He traveled throughout the Balkans and deep into Russia and Turkey, where he bought animal gut for his string instruments. From humble origins he created a small empire. Members of the local guild built the cellos and violins, and Woldemar sold them all over the continent and later worldwide. Each of his six children inherited 100,000 Reichsmark, a fortune at the time, which they soon lost in post-World War I inflation and the bank crash of 1929. He served as the official provider of string instruments to the court of King Albert of Saxony in Dresden, who awarded Woldemar with the Iron Cross First Class. In a twist of history and irony, Mr. Cello emerged a relative—for Woldemar is also my daughter's great-great-great-grandfather.

Dear Woldemar, if indeed you helped give birth to Mr. Cello, he wants you to know he has played Dvorak's cello concerto and Ninth Symphony, and he sends you thanks and greetings From the New World all the way back to the old country.

───────────────

Most people love surprises, as long as they are good ones. The greater they are, the more we rejoice. There have been plenty of astonishing scenarios in my medical practice over the years. Two stories in particular come to mind.

A meticulous "history" and a thorough physical examination make for ninety percent of medical diagnoses, without costly and sometimes superfluous blood work, x-rays, biopsies or other procedures. A history involves asking the right questions. Such questions uncover simple but potentially instructive details patients or parents may forget to mention or deem to be unimportant. A good physical examination complements the history. Too often, the test precedes the diagnosis instead of confirming it as it should.

Dominic was a cute four-year-old little boy with strawberry-blond, curly hair and a healthy number of freckles on his cheeks. He brimmed with energy and vigor.

All day long, he had been fine, and when his father brought him to bed in his upstairs room, he looked as healthy and vivacious as ever. As was his custom, his father turned on the night-light and told him one of the short stories that Dominic loved so much before he kissed him goodnight. Dominic pulled his bed sheets over his head because he felt scared when his parents stayed in the living room downstairs. Soon he got hot and started to sweat, so he took off his pajamas and threw them on the floor.

Thirty minutes later, later than planned, his mother came into Dominic's room to give him the usual hug and tuck him in under his blanket one more time. Dominic, who had long been sound asleep, appeared strangely dark. His mother became concerned and switched on the main light in the room.

Her husband heard a gut-wrenching scream, sprinted up the stairs to the second floor and found Dominic dark-blue. Never before had his parents seen anything like it. Heart or lung problems were not part of Dominic's history, but his parents knew his oxygen level had to be dangerously low. Stories in the media of blue babies, of life-threatening asthma attacks and of sudden infant death syndrome flashed through their minds. His mother put a T-shirt and shorts on Dominic while his father dialed 911.

The paramedics recognized the dire situation and transported him to the nearest emergency room. Surprisingly, his breath sounds were clear, and his heart beat just fine. A perfect oxygen level and a normal chest x-ray did not fit the clinical picture. Unsure of what to do but fearing the worst, the emergency room physician contacted the children's hospital more than an hour to the south, which dispatched a rescue helicopter shortly thereafter.

Dominic did not have much say in the matter, but he loudly protested the separation from his parents. They were two nervous wrecks when they sped down south on I-75 in the family car, hoping to find their beautiful son alive by the time they got to the second hospital.

Dominic arrived with a darker blue skin color than the staff in the emergency room had ever seen. A quick glance did not allow the puzzled senior doctor on duty to make a diagnosis, and the normal results of the tests in the outlying hospital made heart or lung diseases unlikely. He speculated his little patient might have ingested a poisonous substance that altered the oxygen-carrying protein in his red blood cells. If that assumption proved correct, his blood should be chocolate brown rather than dark red. He ordered an additional blood examination and a second set of those tests his colleagues had already performed in the referring emergency room.

A young physician in training named Dr. Jones got the assignment to take care of Dominic, who sat bravely on his stretcher and watched the commotion around him.

"Hi sweetheart, how are you doing?" Dr. Jones asked.

"Fine," Dominic answered truthfully.

"What's your name?"

"Dominic."

"That's a nice name. I'm Dr. Jones. I need to take off your shirt for a moment."

Dominic allowed the doctor to pull his shirt over his head. Dr. Jones put her stethoscope on Dominic's dark blue, almost purple chest. "Take a few deep breaths."

Dominic did not know what deep breaths were and continued to breathe the only way he knew how to.

"Like this, sweetheart." Dr. Jones opened her lips, took in a deep breath and exhaled for Dominic to see and hear. Dominic tried and did a good job. His lungs sounded very clear.

"Now lean forward so I can listen to your back."

Dominic knew what leaning forward meant and complied. Dr. Jones came across as a trustworthy doctor. So far, she had not poked him with a needle. Everybody else had.

"Wow! Jeez! Come look at this," Dr. Jones yelled into the hallway, scaring Dominic. The attending physician, two nurses and a respiratory therapist came running into the room.

Dominic looked blue in the front. His back, however, revealed a healthy pink color. Multiple times people asked him to lean forward and backward so they all could assess the little chameleon. One of the physicians ran his finger down the demarcation line between the two colors.

"What on earth happened to him?" one of the amazed members in his audience questioned.

"Looks like he got painted."

"How? Why?"

Dominic's nurse brought a warm wet cloth and washed away the blue color on his front body and cured his "disease".

His mother had put a new set of bed linens on Dominic's bed that afternoon. The top sheet was dark blue, the bottom sheet white. Dominic's sweat leached out the dye of the linen and stained his face, neck and the rest of his body down to his feet.

When his parents arrived, they were told to take Dominic back home. The ER could do nothing more for him. His father laughed and his mother cried.

I never asked who paid for the helicopter and ambulance rides, two ER visits, two chest x-rays and a few other things essential to Dominic's recovery. His HMO must have had a fit when they got the bills.

———

Vernon always came across as a quiet boy with a shy and hesitant demeanor. His eyes never expressed any emotion other than fear, pain or suspicion. His pediatrician found a painful lump under Vernon's arm, suspected an infection of the lymph glands, and treated him with antibiotics. After a week of no improvement but continued growth of the lump, he referred Vernon to a surgeon, who biopsied the mass. It turned out that in Vernon's case, an unusual, localized form of leukemia had crept out of nowhere; the bone marrow and the blood were not involved. At a later point, he also developed a lump in his pelvis. On both occasions, he showed a short-lived response as chemotherapy melted away the swollen nodes. Such treatments would not likely keep the disease at bay for long, let alone cure it. A transplant represented his best hope for survival and cure.

Shortly before the transplant was scheduled to take place, he spiked high fevers once again. Another recurrence of his leukemia would have been an insurmountable setback because it would have made him ineligible for the transplant.

A simple virus infection could also explain his problems. His physical examination revealed normal findings, but because he had come with a lump twice before, I wanted to make sure he had not developed yet another such lesion elsewhere in his body. The radiologist reviewed the findings on Vernon's CAT scans with me.

"I don't see anything except for this lump in the groin. Sure looks like recurrent disease if you ask me," he said, pointing to the abnormality on the scan.

"That's bad. I just examined him," I admitted sheepishly. "I don't understand how I could have missed this. The way this scan looks, it should have been obvious."

"Maybe it developed very rapidly. You know better than I how fast these things grow."

"I checked him this morning. They grow fast, yes, but not that fast."

"What are you going to do for him now?"

"I have no idea. You know we wanted to transplant him. There's not much sense in doing that in full relapse. His chances of survival long-term would only be ten or fifteen percent, at best."

"Doesn't sound good, does it?"

"I don't want to face his father; he'll be devastated."

"I'm sorry."

"I know, thanks," I said, unsure of how to tell Vernon or his father.

I had missed the lesion. I thought I had been extra careful to not overlook the smallest lump. Like a criminal drawn to the site of his crime, I returned to the place of my defeat. Vernon lay in his bed, glancing at the ceiling.

"Vernon, I'm sorry. I have to check your groin."

"Why? You just did that. Something wrong?" The tone in his voice and his frightened eyes revealed his suspicion. I avoided facing him.

"Did my CAT scan show something?" he asked. His sixth sense allowed him to smell trouble a mile against the wind.

"It wasn't normal," I confessed.

A first tear rolled down Vernon's cheek. I pulled off the bed covers. Vernon lay quietly, eager to monitor the slightest move on my part.

The mass in his groin had vanished. I could see or feel nothing to indicate what the CAT scan demonstrated, and that flustered me.

"I'm not sure Vernon, this feels normal. According to the scans, you have a big lump right here." Vernon wanted to feel for himself.

"Exactly in this area," I said, guiding Vernon's hand to the specific site.

"Feels normal to me," Vernon countered. For the first time in a long while, his voice exuded a hint of optimism.

"To be honest, to me too. How can you explain that?"

"I don't know."

"Does your testicle sometimes come up high?"

"I don't know," he said. That must have been a weird question for him.

"I tell you what. We'll repeat the study."

"The whole thing?" he asked anxiously.

"No, not the whole thing. A quick look here in your groin, that's it."

After that repeat examination, I returned to the radiology suite. "Mike, that kid is completely normal," I told the radiologist. He had already moved on to a few other studies, which he needed to interpret.

"Which one?"

"The kid with the abnormal groin. I can't feel a thing. Can we look at the films? I wonder whether you can see the testicles."

"Sure, but I don't think we looked that far down." The films did not show the area of interest.

"Can we do one or two cuts through that area?"

"If you want to," he answered. "Why do you think it'll look different this time?"

I gave him my reason.

Mike shook his head. "You guys! OK, send him down."

The repeat CAT scan showed a normal groin. The culprit was Vernon's testicle, which this time he had firmly held down in his scrotum.

"Vernon, everything looks normal now," I explained to him half an hour later.

"You scared me," he said quietly.

"I'm so sorry."

"That's OK. It wasn't your fault."

I was grateful for this teaching lesson. It provided another reminder to never take anything for granted in medicine. The things, they are deceiving.

THIRTEEN

DR. DOOM AND DR. GLOOM

It is so mysterious, the land of tears…

ANTOINE DE SAINT-EXUPERY, THE LITTLE PRINCE

I am moved by fancies that are curled
Around these images, and cling:
The notion of some infinitely gentle,
Infinitely suffering thing.

T. S. ELIOT, POEMS

I go,
You stay;
Two autumns

YOSA BUSON, POEMS

Heavy fog hung low above dark, menacing marshes, reducing the sun to a faint and powerless, yellow-gray patch in the hidden sky. Evil spirits lurked unrestrained beneath a thick canopy of oak and birch trees. Sweat-glistened horses panted and neighed above a gurgling, steaming river.

One of more than thirty heavily armed men dismounted and kneeled to inspect the ground. Patches of dry leaves covered moisture-logged soil conspicuously close to the water's edge. He pushed the leaves aside with a careful, swiping motion of his arm. The grin of victory hushed over his face. Underneath the leaves appeared the fresh imprints of the ironed hoofs they had lost upstream on the other bank of the river. The enemy had used the ruse to disguise his trace to no avail.

Full of renewed certainty, he mounted and charged his horse into the forest, leading his men in a stiff gallop southeast. Time finally ran out for his foe. Death or capitulation: those were the alternatives. The end of the war came in sight.

An hour away and on the left side of the river, a smiling, middle-aged warrior rode his beautiful stallion into the northwestern part of the country. Ever aware of imminent ambush or ensnarement, his men often put the irons backwards on the hoofs of his horse. He headed in one direction while the hoofs pointed in the other.

It was the year 777 AD. Once again, Widukind, king of the Saxons, escaped his nemesis, Charlemagne, the king of the Franks.

This favorite legend of my youth came to mind when I met Audrey thirty years after I first heard this story. Never have I been so glad when shown wrong, and so devastated when later proven right, as in Audrey's case.

Audrey's legs rotated outward to such a degree that her feet pointed backward. I thought of her as special for many different reasons, but this particular quality remains indelibly printed in my memory. Audrey started out her existence the wrong way, marched in the wrong direction almost constantly and ended her life the wrong way as well. Yet nobody is better qualified than she is to show the rest of humanity how to live a life the right way.

Audrey had barely celebrated her first birthday when a myriad of symptoms suggested a serious disturbance of her immune system. Her lymph glands were swollen, and her liver and spleen grew to twice normal size. Her marrow contained a plethora of seemingly normal cells engaged in purposeless pursuits detrimental to the rest of her body.

Chemotherapy led to a short-lived improvement but could not cure the disease, and her physicians elsewhere in Florida recommended a marrow transplant. Audrey had no siblings, the most likely individuals to be suitable marrow donors, and neither parent matched her either. A search through the national volunteer donor program identified a suitable individual willing to help as soon as the request came in.

Audrey's doctors removed immune cells from the marrow before infusing it in order to prevent one of the common complications of transplantation. The transplant progressed uneventfully, and the new marrow worked as desired. Audrey would do well as long as her body allowed the marrow to flourish.

Nine months later, her illness reemerged, and her parents transferred her care to our center. Enough cells of her own, old immune system survived the transplant and rejected those of the donor. Further treatment resulted in no improvement at all. Audrey became weak and listless, her body ravaged by her illness. Her parents noticed subtle finger twitching that extended to her right arm and shoulder before generalized convulsions developed. Audrey's eyes rolled upward, her neck stiffened and her arms and legs contracted uncontrollably. The paramedics who came to the home administered Valium, and Audrey stopped seizing for a brief period. In the ambulance, the convulsions started up again.

A doctor in the emergency room injected a second seizure medication, then a third, all without benefit. The multitude of drugs made Audrey too sedated to breathe on her own. The physician inserted a breathing tube into Audrey's lungs and hooked her up to a ventilator. A helicopter brought her to the intensive care unit in our hospital where the seizures continued unabated despite a drug-induced coma. Her spinal fluid showed that the abnormal immune cells had begun to invade the brain tissue and caused the seizures. At this late stage after failure of a transplant, further treatment would be of little use because any improvement, which was unlikely to begin with, would only be temporary.

Chemotherapy injected into Audrey's brain and spinal fluid nevertheless did stop the seizures. She walked out of the hospital on her own strength—a miracle in its own right. The tips of her feet still pointed backward.

Her future remained grim, as much as her recovery gave reason to rejoice. It was only a matter of time until the disease reared its ugly head again.

After Audrey's discharge, her neurologist and I met with her parents to discuss the possibility of a second transplant the family requested. A nurse best summarized the general feeling among the people involved in Audrey's therapy.

"You are not going to transplant her again, are you?" she asked me in private. "Please don't. You know she's going to die."

"I know," I said, "But her parents don't. That's my problem. I don't think they'll agree to let her go."

"Can't you say no to them?"

"That's exactly what I want to tell them. The question is, will they listen?"

The neurologist shared these concerns. Known among the staff as 007 because of his beeper number, he is a more realistic, cautious man than his namesake James Bond. He agreed the risks of a second transplant outweighed the benefits by far. Audrey would crash and burn in the hospital, her life artificially shortened by weeks or months. The goal of a cure remained unrealistic. She would be better off at home, maintaining some quality of life. Risking everything made no sense. The right choice was to forsake the all-out treatment approach.

"What do you mean, you don't want to transplant her?" her mother asked, agitated, as soon as she heard the first cautious words to suggest exactly that. I avoided a direct answer.

"She went through a whole transplant already and yet the disease came right back."

"They took the T-cells out. If they had left them in the marrow, Audrey might have been OK. You said that yourself, didn't you? This time you can leave them in. We'll take that risk."

"It's not about T-cells. It's about all the therapy she's already endured. I told you, patients rarely ever survive a second transplant. And this time we'd have to use total body radiation. There's an incredible risk that her liver or lungs will give out. She could die a horrible death."

"Without the transplant, she'll die a horrible death all the same. I don't see the difference," she burst out.

"Maybe not. Maybe she'll die peacefully. And you'll have quality time at home. Maybe for quite some time, who knows?" 007 added softly.

"Maybe she won't die. You know how stubborn Audrey is. You said so yourself," her father insisted.

"Even if she doesn't die from transplant-related complications, her disease will likely come back," 007 replied.

"There's no question in my mind that we won't cure the disease in her brain," I added.

"You two are Dr. Doom and Dr. Gloom. You have to give Audrey credit. She can do it. I know this," her mother replied.

Before Dr. Doom and Dr. Gloom found words to respond, she added,

"Let me ask you this: what are the chances without a transplant? Zero percent?"

"Short of a miracle, yes. And miracles don't happen too often. I wish they did."

"And with a transplant?" she ignored the response.

"Less than five percent."

"Two percent? Three percent?"

"I wouldn't know for sure."

"But better than zero?"

"Better than zero, yes."

"Then we have to try. We've got to give her that chance. We have to live with this decision for the rest of our lives. You don't."

Neither one of us could dispute that argument.

Six weeks later Audrey walked back into the transplant unit. Radiation therapy led to a massive convulsion. The attending physician on duty that particular night could not contain her anger and frustration, furiously berating Drs. Doom and Gloom.

"See, I told you. You guys are nuts. We should've never done this. She's going down the tubes instead of living and dying with dignity. God have mercy."

I knew she was right. We were nuts. We chickened out when the right thing would have been to stand up to the parents on Audrey's behalf, who could not speak for herself. Now we had come to a point of no return. This was a disaster story in the making.

Except, disaster soon turned into triumph.

Much to everyone's amazement, Audrey did not go down the tubes, no, she actually improved. The events of the following weeks proved her parents correct. Drs. Doom and Gloom, like the rest of the team, could not but rejoice in being proven wrong. Audrey recovered without damage to her brain or to her other organs. The new marrow took hold and she walked out of the transplant unit on her own strength, her feet still pointing backward.

Audrey began to live the normal life she never knew. Every return of her to the clinic reminded a defeated Dr. Gloom of a precious victory. No one represented a better spokesman for the need to persevere despite adversity than Audrey did.

Fast forward a year: a nurse in the office approached one morning, visibly upset. "Have you heard about Audrey?" she asked. The tone in her voice promised nothing positive.

"No. What's going on?" I asked, the sinking feeling of yet another relapse of her disease making the most sense.

"She died last night."

"Oh no, what happened?"

"She fell out of a tree in her backyard."

Her father remained convinced Audrey must have experienced another seizure. Her parents were devastated, but they knew they had given their daughter every last chance in the world.

As absurd as her death appears, as much Audrey's life gives credence to the belief that man can overcome life's limitations and surge beyond all barriers erected for him.

One thing I wonder about: since heaven is a place of perfection, I cannot imagine Audrey with anything other than a strong, elegant stride with legs and feet pointing straight, to the delight of her God who created her.

> Lives of great men all remind us
> We can make our lives sublime,
> And, departing, leave behind us
> Footprints on the sands of time.

HENRY WADSWORTH LONGFELLOW, A PSALM OF LIFE

Few words are more dreaded than cancer. It has always been synonymous with death and dying. The word conjures images of pain and suffering, and of loss and defeat. Blessedly, such pessimism is no longer appropriate in the world of children's cancer medicine. Nowadays, the vast majority of patients, roughly eighty percent, survive and, as adults, most become functioning members of society. Other less well known diseases used to carry an equally grim prognosis, but in many instances, new treatments have dramatically improved the outcome for these disorders. Nonetheless, the growing number of success stories in modern medicine in general and in children's diseases in particular should not create the deceptive impression that failure is no longer possible. Defeat may strike at any time.

In sixteen-year-old Jonathan's case, we failed to take seriously the fact that he lived with more than one enemy. Jonathan expressed a number of features associated with Diamond-Blackfan anemia, a red-blood cell disease named after two Boston physicians. Short stature, a snub nose and an intelligent expression were part of his physiognomy. In contrast, he lacked the wide set eyes and the thick upper lip often associated with this syndrome. Curls of flaming red, Irish hair surrounded an attractive face with tons of freckles and crafty ocean-blue eyes.

He dragged an IV pole behind him while a unit of red blood cells dripped into his vein. Rather than staying in his infusion room as people often asked him to do, he walked around the clinic, preferring the semblance of freedom. Acceptance of authority did not stand high on the list of his priorities.

"I guess you're glad you aren't taking your steroids anymore," I said as he passed by my chair in the outpatient clinic.

"You bet. I'm not taking *those*. No more chipmunks," he added, pulling his cheeks with his thumbs and index fingers so far out that his face gained an expression bordering on the absurd.

I laughed. "You don't have to convince me. May I examine you real quick?"

"Sure," he said, and walked into an empty examination room.

I closed the door and looked him straight in the eye. "How about those other drugs? Are you still doing those?"

Jonathan had avoided eye contact on a few occasions in the past. This time, he returned my look without hesitation. The immediacy and directness of his response assured me he told the truth. "Not any more. I'm clean."

"You're sure? One hundred percent?"

"Sure. One hundred percent."

"I'm glad you told me. You know we've been worried about you."

"I know."

Jonathan came with his fair share of inborn medical problems; a few others he created himself. For a while, he took not only his prescribed medications but a few illicit drugs as well. He knew life almost exclusively from the perspective of a patient, as his problem became abundantly clear within a few months from birth. His marrow did not produce enough red blood cells, whereas the production of the white blood cells and platelets continued in the normal fashion. None of the treatment alternatives offered a good quality of life. Transfusions resulted in the perilous accumulation of iron in his heart and liver, while nightly infusions of another medication under the skin, designed to rid his body of the excess iron, were cumbersome and painful.

Steroid therapy, the sole alternative, led to considerable weight gain. He developed an ugly moon face and a potbelly, side effects he loathed as soon as he became conscious of his appearance. Over the years, he tried both therapies, each with complications. The occasional marijuana and cocaine use became a troublesome outlet for his life's burdens and worries.

"How are things in school?"

"All right," he shrugged.

"That's all you can tell me?" In my experience, one-word answers often disguise more than they declare.

"B's and a few C's."

"I bet your mom is pleased with you."

His smile and nod went hand in hand. "I think so."

"You know it hasn't always been that way," I said, expressing my concern by tilting my head slightly.

He understood perfectly. "I know. I'm better now."

"You sure have come a long way."

It was obvious he agreed. With a big grin he countered, "I wanna go to college."

"Well, I see no reason why you couldn't pursue college if you put your heart and mind to that."

Jonathan smiled his infectious smile, and in my mind I saw him walking across one of the local college campuses already, a big bag of books slung over his shoulder. He always drove himself home upon completion of his clinic visits. At least once every four weeks he returned for further transfusions. Each time, his other blood cell counts came back normal until one day, things changed unexpectedly.

Without warning, his white cells and his platelets plummeted, suggesting complete failure of his bone marrow, a condition known as aplastic anemia. Reports of a transformation from his red cell disease to the much more dangerous new condition did not exist. The textbooks stated it does not happen.

Apparently, Jonathan never read the textbooks, and his marrow in fact showed nothing but empty holes. Further tests shed no additional light on his condition. A marrow transplant would have been the most reasonable therapy, but Jonathan had no suitable donor. Instead, he received immune therapy to reverse the marrow failure, although we did not expect this intervention to normalize the defect in his red cell production. Even if this treatment worked, he could not hope for much more than a return to the monthly transfusions.

"Do you think this will work?" Jonathan asked two months into his new treatment. "I don't like this. My fingers shake all the time and my counts haven't gotten any better." His blood work indicated no response.

"To tell you the truth, we don't know either; sometimes it takes months. You can't expect an immediate response. I sure hope it'll work."

We had difficulty convincing Jonathan to stick with his therapy that ultimately proved unsuccessful. Four months after the start of his new medications, he developed excruciating pain in his belly and lay in his hospital bed, pressing his hands alongside his left flank. A large round mass in his spleen gave reason to worry.

"Do you think this could be cancer?" his mother asked, her hands fidgeting nervously.

"It could be, but it's very unlikely."

"Everything with me is extremely unlikely, but these things happen to me anyway," Jonathan grunted from his bed. Unfortunately, that interpretation barred little correction.

"It could be a lymph cancer or an infection. But they look different on a CT scan. Other cancers don't usually develop in the spleen. It looks like a big old blood clot."

"That's what the surgeon told us, too," the mother confirmed, her face mirroring consolation.

"That's because we looked at the CT scan together, with our radiologists."

"And nobody can tell for sure?"

"I wish I knew somebody who could."

"What are we going to do? Can we take out the spleen?"

"Yes. But that puts Jonathan at risk for infections later. Obviously, we can't put it back into his belly once it's out. If it's a simple blood clot, we'd look pretty foolish. For now, we should treat your pain," I said, turning to Jonathan, "and see how things go."

"What else is going to happen to him when this is over?" his mother asked, exasperated.

"Would you believe me if I told you he'd have no more problems?"

"No!" That shot-gun answer did not surprise me much.

"That's one reason why I wouldn't say it. If we take his spleen out and it's only a bleed, he'd still have his aplastic anemia. And if that were to go away, which it wouldn't, he'd still have his red cell problems."

"I know. I want some hope, you know. We've fought this for so long. Sixteen years. He's never been normal. Everybody says the same thing, and nobody knows. It's so frustrating."

"I'm so sorry." What can you say to someone else whose grief and pain you have never experienced yourself?

The mother did not respond verbally, but she touched my arm, and that touch, brief as it was, spoke of gentleness and care more than words could have conveyed in that moment.

Jonathan went home after moderate improvement. The pain fluctuated, but it never went away completely. Another CAT scan revealed no significant change, which meant we still could not conclusively rule out a serious infection or cancer. His blood counts remained as disappointing as ever, and the benefits of the removal of the spleen began to outweigh the risks of further waiting without a diagnosis.

So, off he went to surgery. What were we going to find? I must confess I was a bit anxious. I did not want to have to face him when he woke up from his anesthesia, and tell him yet another disaster story with miserable implications. He had gone through so much already.

The surgeon did not look all too concerned when he came out of the operating room. Jonathan experienced no complications, and the mass turned out to be nothing but a blood clot. He went home pain free a few days later.

"Tell me this isn't real."

His mother's face expressed part incredulity, part jubilation. Two weeks after his discharge from the hospital, Jonathan's white blood cells and platelets normalized. Even more surprisingly, his red cell count remained stable without transfusions.

"What happened?"

"I wish I knew. We took the spleen out," I said provocatively.

"I know that!"

"Well, that's really all we did."

"What does the spleen have to do with it?"

"Nothing, I would think but I'm not so sure. Maybe everything."

"For four months we do these treatments and nothing happens? And two weeks after the spleen is out, his counts come back normal? That doesn't make any sense, does it?"

I shrugged my shoulders. It did not make a whole lot of sense.

"Does this mean his aplastic anemia is gone?"

"It's possible. It'd be premature to call it that. Something in the spleen may have suppressed his marrow. Now that the spleen is gone, that something is gone, too—but I'm guessing here, you know."

"Now what?"

"We'll wait a while."

Shortly thereafter, all his blood counts normalized, the red cells included.

"How can this be? I thought he was born with this?" his mother asked.

"It doesn't make sense," I had to admit. "But I found one report that described another child with two blood disorders. One was congenital, the other developed later. Both disappeared when they took the spleen out, even the disease present at birth, believe it or not. It's not a whole lot different from Jonathan's case."

"One other case?" his mother asked, ridiculing my research.

"Well, that's all I could find. Are you complaining?"

She laughed. "I know I should be thankful. I just don't understand."

"Honestly, we don't either." One single lucky strike apparently cured two diseases. It felt really good to spread great news, even though we could hardly claim credit for these unusual but fortunate events.

The absence of further blood issues unfortunately did not translate into a problem-free life for Jonathan. The prolonged steroid therapy had weakened his hipbones, which resembled those of a ninety-year-old woman. Hip replacement surgery became unavoidable but he took the renewed hurdle in stride. The lack of need for transfusions made for a superior quality of life, and he graduated from high school with no problems. In fact, he did well for four whole years—or so we believed.

Without rhyme or reason, his red blood cell count dropped again, necessitating renewed blood transfusions. Hepatitis, a serious liver infection, set him back even further. This time, Jonathan wanted treatment by a local adult doctor in Orlando. At the age of twenty-one years, he could claim every right in the world to no longer be considered a child.

His new doctor called the office months later, his voice halting, barely suppressing his emotions. "I wanted to let you know that Jonathan died yesterday."

"I was afraid he wouldn't survive the hepatitis, but this went a lot faster than I thought."

"He didn't have hepatitis. They found him in front of the refrigerator." He stopped there with a pregnant pause.

"Refrigerator? What do you mean?"

"He died from a heroin overdose. They found all kinds of drug paraphernalia on the floor."

We never learned why Jonathan's diseases disappeared upon the removal of his spleen or why his red cell problems recurred years later. We have little choice but to accept what cannot be changed. The past is not preventable, as my son once determined in a moment of introspection. Jonathan's life and death are a good lesson in humility for us and a not so subtle reminder of the limitations of our knowledge. Despite the advances in modern medicine, mankind may never find an end to its search for understanding of who we are.

To this day, a feeling of having failed Jonathan lingers among those who cared for him. We did what we considered reasonable with respect to his marrow conditions—and achieved more than deemed possible. As far as his other problem, we underestimated the demons within him that haunted him for years. We wrote off his addiction as a youthful indiscretion, a compensation for his poor health—until it was too late. Neither Jonathan nor we will get a second chance.

FOURTEEN

JUST A LITTLE LONGER

162

Earth's the right place to love:
I don't know where it's likely to go better.

ROBERT FROST, POEMS

———————————————

A being breathing thoughtful breath,
Traveler between life and death;
The reason firm, the temperate will,
Endurance, foresight, strength, and skill;
A perfect woman, nobly planned
To warn, to comfort, and command;
And yet a spirit still, and bright
With something of angelic light.

WILLIAM WORDSWORTH, SHE WAS A PHANTOM OF DELIGHT

I was in the dog house. Big time. And for good reason.

My wife and I planned to spend a few days in the Smoky Mountains National Park. We packed a beautiful lunch, brought a gallon of water, and drove through Cades Cove, the isolated valley known for its abundant wildlife, gorgeous mountain vistas and preserved homesteads of yesteryear. An hour and a half later, we finally arrived at the trailhead to the Gregory Bald Ridge trail, our destination for the day. In late June, the mountain summit displays a dazzling array of flame azaleas in every hue and provides views almost into eternity.

Eleven miles on foot lay ahead of us. The weather forecast predicted excellent conditions. I grabbed the water from the trunk, and then my stomach sank to my knees. The bag with sandwiches, fruit and trail mix was gone. Actually, it was not gone; it just never came along with us. It sat in the refrigerator back at the condominium where I had blithely forgotten it. My wife joyfully asked whether I had everything. What choice did I have but to confess my inexcusable stupidity?

"How could you forget that?" she asked, her voice betraying anger and frustration. "We can't hike eleven miles in the mountains with no food," she added with a good measure of despair.

I felt miserable. "I don't know," I said sheepishly.

"What are we going to do?" she wanted to know. "We'll never get up there and back without supplies. It's already noon and we haven't eaten any lunch yet."

I felt guilty, having ruined what promised to be a perfect day. I prayed a quick, silent prayer. God, help us please. Not much more than that. I didn't know what else to pray. Manna from heaven? My wife, who remained unaware of my silent conversation with the Lord, suggested prayer. I dutifully agreed. She prayed her prayer out loud, and I could hear in her voice that her anger slowly evaporated. "Come on, let's go," she challenged me after she finished the prayer.

"I don't think that's a good idea."

"We've come this far already. We'll just start walking and see how it goes. We can always turn back."

Her determination impressed me, although I still wondered whether our endeavor now amounted to utter foolishness. We made good progress on the trail with my wife storming ahead and myself wondering how long that would last.

"How are you doing? Wouldn't it be better if we turned around?"

"I'm fine," she answered, still proceeding without looking back to me. "Just a little longer."

We must have covered two to two and a half miles when I heard unusual sounds coming from behind our back. Turning around, I saw four horseback riders coming up the trail, the horses advancing with swift strides. My wife had not yet noticed them.

"The four horseback riders of the apocalypse are coming for us," I called out to her, trying to lighten the mood. They seemed to have prepared for the worst as they wore thick leather coats and boots and would have weathered a thunderstorm of any magnitude. The two of us in shorts and T-shirts looked rather skimpy in comparison.

My wife entertained thoughts of a less biblical, more pragmatic sort. "You ask them whether they have any food. You owe me that," she said, thus giving me an opportunity for redemption. Explaining our plight, I asked for a few spare crackers, temporarily suppressing my embarrassment. Instead of a meager ration, we received a veritable feast. The riders' generosity knew no boundaries, for they pulled from their pockets crackers, cheese, ham and oatmeal bars without hesitation. Needless to say, I thanked them profusely. Greatly invigorated, we barreled up the mountainside behind the horses. On the summit, majestic views far into Georgia, Tennessee and the Carolinas rewarded my satiated wife and an ever grateful husband.

A year later, we came back to the park. This time we started from Clingmans Dome, the highest point in the Smokies, and headed south along the ridge towards Silas Bald. I must have checked twenty seven times to make sure we brought our food with us. Ravenous as bears, we scarfed down our lunch on a sun-drenched meadow overlooking the Tennessee plains, leaving two of the most sumptuous chocolate power bars for dessert and reward at the end of our hike. Deceptively blue skies above suggested a harmless afternoon, but in the distance ominous clouds ballooned, drifting ever so slowly into our path. Halfway towards our goal we realized we'd never reach the bald unscathed. Retreat was the only option. We made it back to a shelter on the tail end of a drizzle moments before the sky turned black and a deluge crashed down all around us.

Twenty minutes into this downpour, a shell-shocked young couple huddling under a ridiculously small umbrella arrived at the lean-to. They had been hiking under the erroneous assumption that they were on a—non-existent—loop trail, and unknowingly moved further and further away from their starting point. In the raging storm they lost all orientation. My wife explained the geography and offered to hike back with them to the parking lot where we had all left our cars, once the storm subsided.

Wesley and Annabel, our new companions, worked as counselors in a Christian youth camp down in the valley on the North Carolina side and wanted to explore the Smokies on one of their few afternoons off.

As fast as the skies blackened in the storm, they now reverted back to their original blues. Slogging through mud and puddles previously known as a trail, my wife who led the pack suddenly asked one of her cut-to-the-chase questions:

"Annabel, are you hungry?"

No, I wanted to shout, *don't ask her that. We only have the chocolate power bars left. Not those!*

Annabel did not respond, even though she must have heard clearly. Whether she was scared or simply embarrassed, I didn't know. No answer, no bars. As simple as that. Our dessert would be safe.

"Annabel, say yes!" my wife broke the silence, taking matters in her own hands. *Oh no. Wasn't it enough that you asked her? Did you have to answer for her, too?* I wanted to complain.

Annabel voiced a timid yes and admitted they were starving. The chocolate power bars! Out they came, one for Annabel, the other for Wesley.

There were no horses on the trail, but the horseback riders from a year earlier, who helped prevent our own little apocalypse—a prayer answered, a gift from heaven—burst into my memory. What a joy it was to see the smiles on our friends' faces as they delighted in our bars—and to relive that memorable rescue from a year earlier. I felt chastened for having been so stingy with our food when others so clearly showed a need that we could so easily provide.

We prayed, and I am quite sure Wesley and Annabel did, too, when things turned unexpectedly scary up in the mountains. The Lord responded to our prayers, and he did so in astonishing, memorable ways.

Prayer *is* powerful. One of the most profound questions, one of our acquaintances told us, came from the mouth of a six-year-old girl. Is it OK to talk to God even when I'm not praying, she reportedly asked with the most sincere and inquisitive expression.

God's ears are always open, and he encourages us to ask for our needs. We better heed caution, though, and consider what it is we are asking for. He may well answer.

Read on for another answered prayer.

Perfection would have been an understatement, and to describe Skylar's head as beautiful would have been an injustice. Michelangelo himself might have chiseled it out of the richest, pearly-pink marble from the quarries of Carrara. Not a single hair disturbed the immaculate, shiny baldness that could have served as a mirror had the skull been flat. Most conspicuously, stern gray-blue eyes splurged color in a face Renoir, Klimt or Picasso in his early days might have painted for eternity. Thin dark brows swerved far out beyond the angle of the eyes before they curved upward in undisguised dissent. She possessed prominent cheekbones that suggested determination and tenacity. The nose swung down with the elegance of a Dorian column. Her pursed, pale lips hid rows of flawless teeth destined to intimidate as much as to chew.

Skylar said she was going to her senior prom "like this". I wasn't sure I had understood her correctly.

"You are not going to wear a wig or a scarf?" I asked naively, expecting a "yes, of course".

Skylar's eyes sparkled in protest. She must have faced that question before.

"No," she countered sharply without giving her response a second thought, "If they don't want to look at me, they don't have to. They can look somewhere else. I don't care."

Her outburst of anger startled me when I shouldn't have been surprised at all. I had known her for over a year, long enough to know that Skylar definitely meant what she said. I should have anticipated her reaction and not asked the question, but then any question or comment with Skylar represented a dangerous undertaking. I could never tell whether she would laugh in agreement, grunt in protest or explode in a rush of anger.

Though still in high school, Skylar already worked part-time as a model. She earned money in a few local jobs and caught people's attention. Before long, she signed a contract with an agency in New York City. That's where she belonged, she told anyone who would listen—in the big, wide world that beckoned so loudly and tugged on her from afar. Beyond the horizon, beyond the provinciality of her hometown—as she experienced it—lay promise and opportunity. She was made for that, craved it, breathed it and exuded it.

Skylar brought a date to her senior prom. The young man did not mind her baldness—at least that is what he told her. Had he not taken her to the event, Skylar would have easily found someone else. Going by herself would not have been a big deal for her, either.

After the prom, Skylar brought a photo of herself and her date. A long black gown accentuated her uncovered head. She looked stunning and determined, her date unsure. He may have had a hard time keeping up with Skylar.

At the beginning of her journey, suffering from fever, aching bones and bruises, Skylar found herself in the clutches of lymphoma. The thought of losing her hair terrorized her. But she also worried about the effects of her therapy on the rest of her body. She feared her treatments might leave her physically unable to pursue the career she had dreamed of since her early childhood. And she distrusted the promise that the appearance of most patients remains unaffected long-term.

In Skylar's case, concerns for her future well-being were not unfounded. Several features of her lymphoma suggested a higher than average risk for recurrent disease. A preliminary search for a marrow transplant donor identified her fraternal twin sister as a perfect match. The family considered that match a life insurance policy, hoping they would never have to make use of it.

Months into her therapy, Skylar presented with symptoms of a sinus infection. Antibiotics brought no relief, and then a CAT scan showed a mass in the back of her nose, a lymph node cancer different from the original one.

Two cycles of more aggressive therapy melted the mass away. Differences in opinion as to the best treatment of these separate cancers made for a confusing scenario for the family.

"I don't want a transplant. I don't like what it's going to do to me," Skylar declared.

"You may not be able to have children of your own. That's certainly a possibility. You might have to take steroids for a while, depending on how well you and your sister match."

"You said we were complete matches," she burst out in opposition.

"You are, but only as much as we can test for in the laboratory. There are other cell structures the two of you may not share. They may be different enough to cause problems."

"I took steroids when I first came here."

"I know."

"I got fat. And I got pimples." No sense in arguing—she spoke the truth. "I don't want to do it." End of that story. Skylar continued with standard therapy.

Several months later, Skylar complained of belly pain.

"What do you think this can be?" Skylar's mother asked. Nothing good came to mind.

Skylar looked eight months pregnant. Instead of carrying a baby, she presented with a mass in her pelvis the size of a soccer ball. Its appearance did not allow us to determine its origin or any relationship to the normal organs. Somewhere in the middle lay a normal uterus. Her normal blood counts and bone marrow did not preclude recurrent lymphoma.

"Do you think the surgeon can cut it out, and she can continue with her treatments?"

If it were only that easy, I thought, before I responded, "I don't think it'll work that way. First we have to find out what it is."

The surgeon opened Skylar's belly with a cut from her belly button down to her pelvis. Half of the mass jumped out at her like a spring-loaded clown's head bursting from a toy box. The ovaries, grown to monstrous size, burst full of lymphoma, abutting each other and simulating a single mass. The surgeon took out the right ovary before she could manage to close the belly for all the pressure, leaving the left ovary behind to allow Skylar to hopefully have normal female hormone levels and become pregnant in the future.

"Does she still have a chance if she gets a transplant?" Skylar's mother asked after the operation.

"If she responds to radiation and more chemotherapy, she has a chance. Not a great chance but still. It's worth a try."

Chemotherapy and radiation led to a rapid decrease in the size of the remaining ovary, and the bone marrow transplant from her sister went well initially. Mouth sores were minor, and her spirits held up.

But fourteen days after the marrow infusion, Skylar took a turn for the worse. She developed fevers and low oxygen and worked harder and harder to breath. Chest x-rays showed hazy lungs. The slippery slope of a relentless downturn became steeper and steeper.

Her mother sat at her bedside when the intensive care doctor prepared to hook Skylar up to a breathing machine. Skylar was scared but well aware she could not breathe on her own for much longer.

"Honey, I'm right here with you," her mother tried to comfort her. "It's only temporary. You won't have to fight so hard, and when your lungs get better, they'll take you off the machine."

Skylar gasped for air in between her progressively shorter sentences. She had so much left she needed to say.

"Don't waste your breath, Honey. Everything will be all right. Daddy is on his way."

"I love you." Skylar mouthed the words with her lips.

"I love you, too," her mother answered with tears in her eyes.

Skylar did not hear her mother's reply as the first sedative engulfed her brain in a deep fog.

"You think she'll be OK?" Her mother's voice contained no illusion. The answer to that question was simple, clear cut and brutal. At that time, marrow transplant patients in need of a breathing machine rarely survived. Too many things have typically gone wrong by the time the lungs fail. In the preceding six years, no such patient in our center lasted more than five or six weeks. The outcome proved so dismal that we entertained the idea of discouraging parents from considering the use of a breathing machine altogether. When

Skylar's lungs failed, nobody found the strength and conviction to suggest to her family to let her go peacefully.

Skylar received twenty-two medications at a time. We discussed the possibility of a lung biopsy, but set aside that idea. Skylar was too unstable for the surgery, and no one could think of a condition for which we had not already implemented some form of treatment on an empirical base.

Skylar's condition deteriorated, and the breathing machine provided more and more breaths every minute, more pressure and more oxygen. The ultimate outcome and the signs of defeat shone clearly as a full moon on a cloudless night. Soon we expected to reach a point where we had given everything technically and humanly feasible to support her life. Her other organs showed the growing strain as she needed medications to keep her blood pressure up and others to urinate. The news from the intensive care team became increasingly desperate, and the team of nurses and physicians involved in her care who had been traveling this journey with her for many years began to discuss turning off the breathing machine as the only merciful solution. The hospital chaplain prepared the parents for the inevitable.

"Just a little longer," the mother requested, hoping for the unrealistic, the impossible. She was not yet ready to give up on Skylar, her baby. Skylar was supposed to have her life ahead of her, not behind her already.

The first positive sign, a need for less oxygen, elicited an attitude of disbelief on my part, for fear of false hope. Her kidney function improved. The strain on her heart decreased and the fluid filled, stiff lungs became more compliant. After three and a half weeks on the machine, Skylar came off the ventilator. Tests showed all her blood cells with the characteristics of her sister's. Following another two weeks of recovery, Skylar walked out of the hospital on her own strength.

Life once again looked sweet. A few months at home remained before the big adventure in New York City was to unfold. The mall, the movies, her boyfriend and her car made for the highlights of the spring before graduation.

Two months later, her belly swelled up yet again. The lymphoma returned as if it had never seen treatment, let alone a transplant.

"I don't understand. Why would God do this?" her mother asked. I told her I do not know why God "does" things or allows suffering like her daughter's illness. Then I told her about Mike and Jesus' invitation to meet him in heaven. "She'll be in charge of Mike and the other children up there. She'll be great with the young ones."

Skylar's mother smiled briefly before sadness spread over her face. "But why did he not take her when she got so sick in the ICU? It would have been so much easier."

Why? I wondered myself. God's ways are not ours. I asked her gently, "You're sure it would have been easier? He could have given her back to you so you could say good-by. You have so much you need to talk about."

"I don't know. What am I going to do? What am I going to tell her?"

"You have to tell her the truth like you've always done. It'll be better that way. You'll be there for her when it counts. You've always been there for her."

Skylar's mother told her daughter the truth. Neither one tried to "protect" the other only to hurt her in the process. Skylar had time to say her farewells, but she fought the end as much as she fought everyone and everything else she found unacceptable. Life was too precious to give death any minute more than absolutely necessary. Towards the end, she weakened so much she could not keep her eyes open for long.

Everything of importance had been said. Her mother gave her permission to die. You see, children often refuse to die and will not die unless and until their parents explicitly allow them to go.

"It's OK, Skylar. You don't have to fight any longer. You can let go now." She noted Skylar's feeble attempt to squeeze her hand.

"Just a little longer, mom," Skylar whispered.

When her mother put her face on Skylar's chest, Skylar closed her eyes for the last time.

The way I understand the Bible, we will all have new bodies in heaven: healthier, longer-lasting ones—after all they have to be good enough for eternity—but I would not be surprised if Skylar turns heads even up there. Perhaps she'll be blessed with a bit more patience, especially if indeed she is now in charge of the little ones, like Mike. She'll do a fantastic job.

JUST KIDDING

We are not here to play, to dream, to drift;
We have hard work to do, and loads to lift;
Shun not the struggle - face it; 'tis God's gift.

MALTBIE DAVENPORT BABCOCK, BE STRONG

Most hospitals in this country have medical conferences, which provide a place and time for learning, development of new ideas and patient care planning in difficult cases. They also present a forum to disagree. That kind of discourse sharpens people's minds.

On one of these occasions, a colleague made an off-the-cuff, not very sensitive remark. Almost everyone laughed, but it caused an irate response from one of the younger physicians in training. In the end we could all agree on this: humor is one of our greatest friends. This holds true especially for those of us who are working in the trenches of cancer warfare. The witty and tongue-in-cheek responses of caregivers and even more so of patients to their ordeals and circumstances are particularly welcome. Many times such interactions have brightened my otherwise dreary day.

Flight 576 from Tampa to Dallas took off into the beautiful, cloudless Florida sky and reached a cruising altitude of thirty-one thousand feet after twenty minutes. When the pilot turned off the seat belt sign, one of the passengers, a young man with a scrubby hint of a beard and shoulder-length hair, got up from his seat. He stood in the center aisle, grabbed his hair and pulled a lock out of his scalp.

"Oh no," he said loud enough for the passengers next to him to notice. He held up the lock in one hand and grabbed more hair with the other. "What's going on?" Several rows of passengers turned to him. After he dropped both handfuls of hair to the floor, he snatched another bushel from the back of his head. The hair diminished as rapidly as the bald spots grew. He looked around in anguish. "What's happening to me?" He pulled more bushels of hair with frantic gestures and held them towards the stewardess who had noticed the commotion in the center aisle.

"Sir, are you all right?" she asked with the gravest concern in her voice.

The young man ignored her question. Instead, he held a bushel towards her. She stepped back, horrified. He threw the hair on her shoes before he pulled more from the top of his head. The stewardess bristled, as if she suspected a deadly infection she was certain to contract if she came any closer.

"I've never seen anything like this," she stammered. "I think I better notify the captain," he heard her say.

Matt, the young man, had recently celebrated his twentieth birthday. Life proved difficult enough that others in similar situations might have thrown in the towel, but the thought of giving up never crossed his mind.

Instead of finding respite from his most recent challenges, he now faced the next hurdle. A lump above his collarbone had developed over a few months. The lump did not bother him much initially because it did not cause any pain. Then he began to cough as the lump grew to the size of a golf ball and another one developed in his chest.

Matt's tumor, a cancer known as Hodgkin lymphoma, extended from the neck to the middle of his chest. At the beginning of his ordeal he underwent chemotherapy, with radiation to follow later on. The illness posed yet another hurdle in a never-ending series of troubles, another monkey wrench thrown in between the spokes of the wheels of his young life. He decided to proceed with his therapy, get it over with, and get on with it. As if he had another choice. If everything went well, he would finish in six months.

The first course of chemotherapy progressed as expected. He could deal with the bouts of nausea. During the second cycle, Matt noticed the first few hairs falling out. He knew he would lose all of them but did not mind as long as they grew back.

After discharge from the hospital, he wanted to visit relatives out of town. Matt was inspired to take a course of action only when he boarded the aircraft on the tarmac in Tampa. Few other opportunities were going to present themselves to him to put a stamp of his own making on this otherwise so miserable endeavor. After all, he still maintained some control over his life, but soon enough, it would be too late. He would not suffer his fate; no, he would take it plainly in his hands.

"This sucks, doesn't it?" he said to the flabbergasted stewardess, with his dark, phlegmatic voice. Almost completely bald, he held a last bushel of hair in his hands.

"See what chemotherapy does to you? Ridiculous. I don't even wanna know how I look like," he added before he calmly sat down and browsed through the airline's in-flight magazine, ignoring the consternation of those around him.

"You are *cute*," fifteen-year-old Michelle yelled across the room. She never minced words. I must admit I had blushed the first time she told me this in front of half of our clinic staff. Since then she has said the same thing at least ten times. I quickly figured out that Michelle finds everyone with a Y-chromosome attractive. Her raging hormones explained her behavior. Recently she was beside herself when she saw her favorite movie star in California, and for weeks nobody else deserved the attribute "cute". But now, apparently, her memory had faded, and I joined the rank of the cute once more, for the moment at least.

Michelle is a nice girl, without question, although she is a complicated young lady. She has an insufficiency of her adrenal gland, low blood platelets, a kidney tumor and, to top it off, Down syndrome. None of these illnesses set her back. She remains astonishingly assertive and demanding. She always knows exactly what she wants—and she usually gets it.

I like Michelle, but despite my tender feelings for her I try to keep a distance between her and myself now. You see, Michelle loves ties. I usually wear a tie to work. If within arm's reach, she pulls on it and kisses it. She has almost knocked me off my feet on a few occasions. At first, it did not bother me.

However, the last time I allowed her to kiss my tie, and did not pay enough attention, she suddenly used it to blow her nose. An explosion of snot blanketed and obscured my tie and shirt. By the time I realized what was happening, I had lost the opportunity to intervene and prevent the disaster. I stood too stunned and speechless to be upset, but I was a mess and needed to wear an OR scrub for the remainder of the day. No more tie kissing for Michelle, not anymore.

Kathryn was everything Greg had always wanted in a girlfriend. She looked pretty and was highly intelligent, but above all, he appreciated her exuberance and cheerfulness. Greg could imagine spending the rest of his life with her—if only she returned his affection with the same fervor.

A stud pierced the left side of Kathryn's nose. *Such a pretty face shouldn't be marred like that,* he thought. *This concept of beauty in the eye of the beholder is all nonsense.* Most of her friends were metal aficionados and had encouraged her to get her "adornment". The abundance of metal studs and rings up and down their ears and noses was an uphill battle for him.

Greg could not deny a deep aversion to anything metal after years of therapy for an aggressive leukemia. Needles were made of metal; needles hurt; and he had encountered them way too often over the last two and a half years. He could not remember how many times he endured blood draws, bone marrow aspirates and spinal taps. He did not understand how anyone in his right mind could ever have his body pierced voluntarily.

Greg and Kathryn, both freshmen at the University of Florida, attended two classes together. He did not feel comfortable enough, barely a month into their friendship, to talk about the treatment for his leukemia he had recently completed. His doctors gave him a clean bill of health during his last visit. His hair grew back thick and with a lighter, more attractive color than he remembered from the time before his diagnosis.

But Kathryn did not yet need to know; he worried how she might react to such a revelation. When he started chemotherapy and lost his hair, people kept a distance as if they feared contracting a deadly disease. The epithets of "skinhead" or "weirdo" stung him and now motivated him to keep his past quiet for a while longer. Ultimately, of course, he would tell her. The only thing that might give away his secret was his port, an intravenous device implanted under the skin of his chest wall. The removal of the device needed to wait until the end of the semester when he planned to return home. He grew another inch and gained a few pounds, and because of his weight lifting, he developed strong pectoral muscles. Nobody noticed the abnormality of his chest as long as he kept his shirt on.

One Friday afternoon, Greg mustered the courage to ask her out to dinner. Pizza and a coke seemed an innocent enough proposal. To his great disappointment, Kathryn had already made plans for the evening, having promised other friends to meet with them in a local hangout, but she encouraged him to join her. Of course, she said, her friends wouldn't mind if he came along.

When Greg arrived, Kathryn and six of her friends already sat around a small table, and she introduced him to the group. The others hardly took notice and continued their conversation. The first home game of the Gators, the heavily favored local football team, was scheduled for the following day. Everyone carried an opinion and everyone had tickets, except Greg who had neither since he didn't really care much about football. He sat quietly, limiting his participation in the conversation to an occasional nod while throwing furtive glances towards Kathryn that went unnoticed. Already he thought of the evening as a waste.

When the issue of college football ran its course, he became more optimistic. In due time, the conversation might gravitate toward a topic to which he could contribute in a way that might impress Kathryn. His hopes were dashed when the girl next to him blurted:

"Did you guys know Jerry got his tongue pierced?" All eyes turned to Jerry.

"Let's see!" one of the other girls called out. Jerry stuck out his tongue. The upper pole of his metal adornment protruding through his tongue struck the back of his upper front teeth, producing a clicking, snapping sound. Jerry pulled his tongue back in his mouth and grinned. Greg was disgusted.

"Cool," said one of the girls.

"Wow," added another.

"Any others?" Kathryn wanted to know.

Jerry shook his head. "Not yet," he responded.

Bob, the other male at the table, pulled up his T-shirt and presented his own metal-perforated nipples. "I got these last week. Twenty bucks."

This is ridiculous. You guys are nuts, Greg thought to himself, forgetting Kathryn momentarily.

"Where?" Jerry asked. Bob mentioned the name of a place on the other side of town.

"Too expensive. Over at Harry's, its only fifteen. Eighteen max," one of the girls interjected.

"Seriously?"

Greg sat speechless. Kathryn had forgotten about him. She had not acknowledged him once in the last five minutes. Even if he was not bashful, he could not participate. It was a moot point: he could not show rings, studs, anything of value in their eyes. Nothing.

Except…

He jumped to his feet, toppling his chair in a loud crash. Exclaiming a forceful "Look at this," he grabbed his shirt along the button line with both hands and ripped it open. All eyes turned to the hump under his chest.

"Man…" one of the girls said, impressed.

"Wow," said the girl who had commented similarly when Jerry showed his tongue.

"Can I feel?" the third girl asked admiringly. One after the other, the girls touched his chest. Kathryn's hair smelled wonderful when she came close to him.

"Where can I get one of these?" one of the girls wanted to know.

"I've never seen one like that," Jerry added, pursing his lips. "Looks like the power hump of a Mitsubishi."

His tongue could not compare with Greg's device, nor could the others demand attention any longer. Kathryn looked at him with admiration, and Greg glowed. He kept his secret for the moment.

After the game the next day, Kathryn and Greg did go out for pizza, and this time, she had eyes only for him.

180

SIXTEEN

CUT IT OUT

Suddenly a sound like the blowing of a violent wind
Came from heaven and filled the whole house
Where they were sitting.

ACTS 2:2

Early spring in Florida brings balmy, pleasant days. It could have been a marvelous Sunday morning. I did not have to work, I had a good night's sleep and a great breakfast, and a slight breeze coming in from the Gulf of Mexico should have been plenty of reason to cherish a new day; and yet I steamed with anger. My wife worshipped in church while I sat outside in our family car, fuming and brooding. Church was not for me. Organized religion exemplified the last thing I had any reason or desire to engage in. Faith and belief in my opinion back then only served the fainthearted, who could not control their own lives. They were for those that hoped for relief of their problems by a power that did not exist.

The only reason I even came close to a church building was my wife's debilitating eye injury and her powerlessness to drive the car herself. Our young daughter had crawled into our bed one morning a few days earlier and accidentally scraped a good chunk of my wife's cornea off her left eye. An hour and a half of worship for my wife made for an hour and a half of misery for me, a process we repeated weeks later when a partially healed cornea sloughed off during REM sleep and sent spasms of pain through my wife once again. This scenario, including my impatient, glum existence outside the church walls, reoccurred four or five more times over the next year and a half before a great eye doctor with access to modern laser technology finally put an end to my wife's suffering.

By that time, I had lost all power of will and finally succumbed to the invitation by several of my wife's acquaintances to visit the church and see what it was all about. People acted very friendly, I admitted halfheartedly. But for their ill-conceived convictions, as I perceived them back then, I did not hold them in high regard. These were amazing people, like the collegiate US ice hockey champion and teacher of high school chemistry in Papua New Guinea before he built a sailboat in Australia by himself and sailed it single-handedly to Florida. Then there was a dentist who led a several-hundred-member Christian organization and repaired the teeth of Maasai children in Kenya. One selfless woman gave hospitality to half the community; another rescued an orphaned girl from China; a third regularly went out of her way to provide transportation for a troubled youth whose only sanity rested in a few hours each week with people who truly cared for him. A schizophrenic who, despite the most horrific voices shaking his body, still managed to rise to his feet on Wednesday night services and quote whole passages from Ephesians or Philippians at the most opportune moments. The pastor, who taught Ethics and Philosophy in a local college to support his family, would later go to the Philippines as a missionary. Not to mention the collegiate US pummel horse champion who managed the affairs of a technical company and the finances of the church at the same time.

My pride knew no boundaries, and neither did their grace, gentleness and friendship for me.

Sunday morning, a few weeks before Easter of '96, our church celebrated communion as it always did, on the first weekend of each month. By that time, I had attended communion eight or nine times, and as on all prior occasions, I would let the bread and the wine pass by because I found little meaning or relevance in this celebration. I was not going to participate in an empty, pointless ceremony to acknowledge a god that no one would ever meet, assuming he existed in the first place.

The trays with bread and wine passed from row to row towards the back of the sanctuary when all of a sudden a harsh, loud wind blew from the rear, brushing my right face and shoulder. The hair on my neck bristled and I froze stiff with fright, but within a second or two, my fear turned into overwhelming joy—for without a kernel of doubt I had met the living God right then and there. At that moment, all my resistance, querulousness, pride, and self-reliance evaporated, replaced by an overwhelming awe and sense of relief. To my astonishment, a crystal clear voice spoke in German, saying: *"Cut it out."* God actually used the words *Nun ist es genug,* literally translated: Now it is enough. Although the sound pierced my ears, no one besides me apparently heard it; my wife to my right, who could not have been more than inches away from the wind, and friends and acquaintances on my left and in front of me continued to listen undisturbed to the worship team's melodious music. None of the others had heard or felt the gust or the voice.

This time, I joined the others in communion and partook of the bread and the wine.

My wife noticed my eating and drinking, and upon hearing what had transpired, told me with tears in her eyes that she had been praying for me the entire service. Later she explained that she had asked the Lord to do for me what he had done for Paul on the road to Damascus.

After the service, our worship leader approached me with grave concern for my wellbeing. "What's wrong with you? Are you all right?" he burst out. He had seen something in my face and noticed my loss of composure, despite the fact that I sat several rows towards the back. He feared great distress on my part and obviously remained entirely unaware of what had happened. I told him I had met the Holy Spirit.

"You have to tell John!" he said.

"I know," I said, and walked over to our pastor.

"Today I took the bread and the cup," I said, almost whispering, overwhelmed by the moment.

John burst out, "Do you know what that means?"

"I know what that means," I answered softly.

"Do you know what that means?" he repeated himself, incredulous.

I did know what that meant. Yet, in a larger sense, I am still learning what that means.

On Easter morning three weeks later I made a public confession of my faith before my family and friends. We gathered at the shores of Tampa Bay when it was still near pitch black for the church's annual sunrise service. Following a wonderful celebration of singing, prayer and a short sermon, seven or eight of us were baptized, the ember-orange-red sun lifting over the horizon in our backs. Walking to the parking lot afterwards, I turned around one more time to take in the momentous morning, noticing a large sign with a city ordinance that prohibited all swimming and bathing because of heavy contamination of the water. Our pastor acted a bit embarrassed but I chuckled. That glorious day, I am convinced, I was immune to E coli or whatever other bugs might have been swimming and preying on the innocent in the polluted waters.

SEVENTEEN

BLIND MAN WALKING

Did you tackle that trouble that came your way
With a resolute heart and cheerful?
Or hide your face from the light of day
With a craven soul and fearful?
Oh, a trouble's a ton, or a trouble's an ounce,
Or a trouble is what you make it.
And it isn't the fact that you're hurt that counts
But only how did you take it?

EDMUND VANCE COOKE, HOW DID YOU DIE?

———————

Miracles are all right, Polly. The only difficulty
About them is that they don't happen nowadays.

GEORGE BERNARD SHAW, ST. JOAN

Friends of ours suggested we see *Facing the Giants,* a movie that found favorable reviews in the local media. It portrayed the unlikely story of a divine-human alliance. A football coach fell on hard times. His world folded in on itself. He came close to losing not only his job but his wife as well, and he did not have the slightest idea of how to fix his personal or professional life. The heart-warming, gut-wrenching prayer he sent to the master-healer above transformed loss and defeat into success and love. It was a good story—too good to be true.

After the credits, outside the theater, my wife and I shared our doubt and disbelief that the God of the universe would so quickly reverse a man's misfortunes.

A lone quarter in the parking lot under a street lamp caught my attention. It was a nice sight, but with that one coin I would not be able to do much of anything. The thought popped into my brain that God could grow it into the movie's entrance fee at the spur of the moment, but he would never enact such an awe-inspiring switch. Truth be told, miracles are rare even for the elect.

A few steps further, to my great surprise, I noted a green-crinkled ten-dollar bill. Not a soul walked anywhere in sight. While sharing these thoughts with my wife, I found more money: a penny with the inscription "In God we trust." When God showed me that quarter of faith, he affirmed he can and does turn the tides—even when, by human criteria, all seems lost.

The odyssey of a little boy from the other side of the world could not show more clearly the Lord's power and compassion.

The clinic had never seen a more hectic morning. The phones rang off the hook. Everyone who called the office wanted their problem solved right that moment. The secretary sounded exasperated. "This lady called for the third time already. She's crazy," she said with a sigh.

"What's going on?" I asked.

"Her nephew has leukemia. She wants you to treat him."

"Novel concept," I said wryly.

Her mouth twisted. "I don't feel like joking."

"A little laugh won't hurt. Nothing wrong with her request, is there? Why isn't he coming?"

"Oh yes, there is. He's in Cambodia. She wants us to get him over here."

"Why don't you fly over and pick him up?"

"I told you she's crazy."

"Is he stable enough to come here?"

"How do I know? I'm the secretary. You're the doc, remember?"

"Funny, funny. Anything else she said?"

"Yeah, he's very sick. She said he's blind because he bled into his eyes." She frowned. "Can that happen?"

"Well, yeah, if he had a bad blood clotting problem, maybe. No platelets, something like that."

"Oh, also, she said he had a stroke. Can't move one side of his body. He can't come here like that, can he?"

"Of course not. He sounds like a train wreck." Someone in such a desperate physical state had no business trying to make a trans-Pacific journey.

"Should I ignore her then, or tell her he should stay where he is?"

"I'll talk to her. I'll tell her to keep the kid local. Probably wouldn't survive the trip over here. Where did she call from anyway?"

"Ocala, I think. She lives here, I guess."

"Can you get her on the phone for me please?"

"Sure, give me a moment."

The woman came across as friendly, soft-spoken and very scared. Her youngest nephew, Mateo, suffered from a particularly aggressive form of leukemia. During the initial treatment he developed a life threatening blood infection and as a result, severe blood clotting abnormalities. She knew he had bled into the brain and into both eyes, making him blind and paralyzed on the right side of his body. As far as she could tell from talking to her sister, Mateo's mother, his condition had stabilized. His physician recommended a bone marrow transplant in the US. Mateo's older sister lived with their aunt in Florida and might be a donor.

"Would you be willing to talk to the doctor in Cambodia if I have her call you?" she asked after she described her nephew's plight.

"I'll talk to him, yes. But I want you to know it will be very difficult to pursue treatment here."

I recited a long litany of challenges to overcome, implying that Mateo's treatment was virtually impossible in our hospital. Without a doubt, other institutions beyond the borders of his country would not want to provide care for him either. He was too ill to travel. The lack of a visa and insurance posed insurmountable obstacles. Simply because he had a sister did not guarantee that he had a matched marrow donor. Regardless of whether our group consented to treating him as a charity case, the hospital would not likely accept him as a patient.

The physician called from Cambodia the following day. The treatment options in Phnom Penh were limited, which prompted her to suggest that Mateo's mother bring her son to the United States. A transplant, which was his best chance for a cure, was out of the question in her country.

Just to get started—in the unlikely event that everything turned out positive—we decided to tissue-type Mateo, his sister, and his mother. In light of a one-in-four chance of a match, the whole venture would likely end at this first crucial step. I promised to contact our hospital with a request for treatment on a compassionate basis. We would have to deal with a long series of administrative hurdles. Deep down I hoped Mateo would stay in his own country. He did not make a good candidate for a marrow transplant, or for that matter, for any other aggressive therapy because of the multiple complications he had suffered already. The hospital would surely nix the plan.

Tissue typing showed the siblings to be a perfect match. Mateo slowly improved but he still could not see or walk. At least he could speak.

The hospital had not responded affirmatively. They were "studying" the case, as one of the administrators said laconically. If they studied long enough, the whole thing would be a moot point.

A few days later, an unanticipated phone call came from Chicago. Mateo's mother had taken matters into her own hands to speed up the process, knowing that time was of the essence in her son's treatment. The longer she waited, the more likely his leukemia would recur, or even another disaster might strike. In a moment of more determination than desperation, she flew

Mateo to Chicago, where a distant relative had suggested urgent help could be found in one of several local university centers.

A pediatric cancer specialist agreed with the Cambodian physician, but the local transplant center rejected Mateo because of a lack of funds. He called us to ask whether we would be willing to accept him for further care.

Unexpectedly, our hospital gave the green light. It decided to honor the family's request because Mateo's sister and aunt lived in Florida. The chief administrator wanted to know whether Mateo had stabilized enough to undergo the transplant.

"He is OK for sure? No other problems we have to worry about?"

Any assumption of stability in a cancer patient is a precarious one. We had to rely on the colleague in Chicago and his assessment of Mateo's condition.

"From what I can tell, he's in good enough shape for the transplant. They looked at his bone marrow one more time a few days ago. He's still in remission. We'd go ahead if he were here."

"Well, all right then. But let me know if anything comes up. Anything!"

Once more, I called the physician up north.

"He's fine. Remission marrow, I guess I told you already. He can't see. Of course, that's never going to change. But that's the only thing. His weakness is getting better," he affirmed.

"No reason not to transplant him, as far as you are concerned?"

"None. Go for it. We are grateful that you'll accept him."

Two days later, a frightened boy arrived in the company of his mother and aunt. Whenever people approached, let alone touched him, he scratched and bit in misguided response. He could not see; his right arm hung limp; and he spoke no English. His horrendous odyssey in Cambodia, travel to the US and the procedures in Chicago scared him to the point of unmitigated mistrust.

"You've got to come and look at his foot right now," his admitting nurse yelled across the hallway.

"What's wrong?"

"It's awful. I've never seen anything like it."

I pulled back the bed sheet and exposed his leg. Five fouling black toes falling off his forefoot came to light. He suffered from gangrene because of his infection in Cambodia. The mother confirmed that it occurred when he bled into his eyes and stroked. Our colleague had calmly neglected to mention this detail in the attempt to get rid of him, the sooner the better. Mateo could not get his transplant as long as the toes rotted off of his foot. They would act as the source of a potentially fatal infection during the transplant when his infection-fighting white blood cells and his immune system hit rock bottom.

Mateo required an amputation of all five toes before he could get any other therapy. The administrator growled, upset, and rightly so. "You said he was OK to proceed to transplantation," he admonished me.

"Well, that's what the guy in Chicago told me. I asked explicitly about potential problems, and he said they didn't know of any."

"One of these days, you'll put us all out of business."

I couldn't tell whether he was serious or only trying to be funny. I could have said something in response but felt compelled to wisely shut up before his patience ran out. Not only did the extra, unplanned surgery pose all sorts of risks and endanger his survival—the delay in definitive leukemia treatment not being the least of these—but from a practical perspective, this unfortunate scenario might threaten any further "charity cases" we or others might want to bring before our hospital administration.

One of our plastic surgeons amputated the toes. The wounds were clean and healed well. Soon thereafter, Mateo underwent his transplant, and he did great. It ended up being relatively cheap to complete, at least compared to other transplants we have performed in the past and to most of those we'll likely do in the future. But we will not accept another patient from elsewhere without first inspecting him or her from the tip of the nose to the toes underneath the socks. Lesson learned!

Before the transplant, an eye surgeon had evaluated Mateo to see whether he could improve his vision but considered surgery unlikely to be of any benefit. After Mateo recovered, another eye doctor tried his best. To our great disappointment, the operations on both eyes failed miserably. Mateo could see nothing but a hint of light. He would live, he would walk with assistance, but he would never see. We wondered what help for blind people might be available in Cambodia if he went back.

Two months later, Mateo returned for a follow-up examination. I stood in the hallway, engaged in a telephone conversation with another physician. The family came through the door of the waiting room, and Mateo walked straight towards the weight scale and the wall. Neither the nurses nor a technician present in the room paid any attention to him, and I feared that Mateo would crash into the wall. Alarmed, I dropped the receiver and yelled out, "Careful, he's going to hurt himself."

Everyone laughed, Mateo's family included. Mateo turned towards me and smiled.

"He can see," his mother replied. "You didn't know?"

I had not been in the outpatient clinic for weeks, and nobody had told me. I was the last to know. All of a sudden, Mateo had begun seeing silhouettes, and finally, everything else. Today, Mateo is in school, and he can read as well as write.

A blind man can see.

Mateo is a blessing to all of us. He has come a long, long way. Not only did he travel half-way around the world. Moreover, for months he walked precariously near death at every step. We feel privileged that God allowed us to accompany him on his journey. Mateo is living proof of what Carl Sandburg once said:

There is only one child in the world, and that child is all children.

Made in the USA
San Bernardino, CA
28 December 2019

62460793R00113